INTEGRATING SCHOOL SUCCESS AND CAREER READINESS

Strategies, Student Activity Sheets,
Tools, and Assessments

by Imogene Forte and Sandra Schurr

Incentive Publications, Inc.
Nashville, Tennessee

Illustrated by Marta Drayton
Cover by Marta Drayton
Edited by Jennifer J. Streams and Angela L. Reiner

ISBN 0-86530-449-1

Copyright ©2000 by Incentive Publications, Inc., Nashville, TN. All rights reserved. No part of this publication may be reproduced, stored in a retrieval system, or transmitted in any form or by any means (electronic, mechanical, photocopying, recording, or otherwise) without written permission from Incentive Publications, Inc., with the exception below.

Pages labeled with the statement ©2000 by Incentive Publications, Inc., Nashville, TN are intended for reproduction. Permission is hereby granted to the purchaser of one copy of **INTEGRATING SCHOOL SUCCESS AND CAREER READINESS** to reproduce these pages in sufficient quantities for meeting the purchaser's own classroom needs only.

PRINTED IN THE UNITED STATES OF AMERICA
www.incentivepublications.com

Table of Contents

Preface 9

Chapter One

**Accommodating Differing Learning Styles, Abilities, and Interests
to Integrate School Success and Career Readiness** 11
    Using Multiple Intelligences
        to Integrate School Success and Career Readiness 12–13
    Multiple Intelligences and Career Chart 14–15

Multiple Intelligence Activities **16–28**
    Exploring the World of Business 16–17
    Understanding Conflicts that Impact the World of Work 18–19
    Pondering Parental Support for Achievement 20–21
    Extra! Extra! Careers in a Book 22–23
    Difficult Employees Can be Difficult to Work With 24–25
    Meeting the Needs of a Happy Employee 26–28
    Interdisciplinary Learning Stations 29–32
    What's Out There For Me? 33-34
    Using the Read and Relate Concept
        as an Instructional Tool 35
    Six Read and Relate Activities 36-38

Open-Ended Self-Evaluation Activities **39–46**
    A One of a Kind, Unique You 39
    Occupations of Interest 40-41
    Visualizing the Future 42-43
    Job Preferences 44
    Personally Speaking 45
    Write and Reflect 46

Chapter Two

**Developing Higher-Order Thinking Skills and Problem-Solving Abilities
to Integrate School Success and Career Readiness** 47
    Using Bloom's Taxonomy to Integrate School Success and Career Readiness 48–49
    Narrowing Work Preferences (Bloom's Taxonomy Activity) 50–51
    What's Your Interest? (Assessing Career Interests/Bloom's Activity) 52–53
    Digging into the Dictionary (Improving Dictionary Skills) 54–56
    Money Matters (Money Management/Bloom's Activity) 57–58
    Business Smarts (Business Structures/Bloom's Activity) 59–60

Finding Out About Your State's Economy (Analyzing State Economy/Bloom's Activity) 61–62
Defining and Diffusing Conflict (Conflict Resolution/Bloom's Activity) 63–64
Investigation Cards 65-66
Investigating the World of Work 67–69
Business in the News 70–71
Using Williams' Taxonomy to Integrate School Success and Career Readiness 72–73

Williams' Taxonomy Activities
How's Your Performance? 74-75
Creating a Climate for Learning 76–77
Looking at Technology 78–79
Technology in the Workplace 80–81
Think About Jobs 82–83
Confronting Conflict 84–85
School Safety and Student Security 86–87

Creative Thinking Exercises
What's Your Opinion? 88
Using Krathwohl's Taxonomy to Explore Gender Issues 89
Quality Counts 90
Reflecting on Grades 91–92
Searching for Feelings 93
Decisions, Decisions 94–95
Goals to Go 96–97
Lists that Inspire Creative Thinking 98–99
21st Century Career Challenges and Choices to Consider 100–101
Exploring Creative-Thinking Challenges Related to School Success 102
Two Sides of Every Career 103
Eliminating the Negatives Related to School Success 104–105
Eliminating the Negative Sack 106

Chapter Three

Using Basic Skills to Integrate School Success and Career Readiness 107
What's the Question? (Sharpening Questioning Skills) 108
Twelve Possible Out-of-School Projects to Sharpen Use of Basic Skills 109–110
Clarifying Predictions (Using the Internet to Verify Predictions) 111
Creative Writing 112
Writing for Success (Checklist) 113
Poetry and the World of Work 114–115
Keeping Up with the World Around You 116–117
World Map 118

Examining a Company's Annual Report (Reading to Find Answers) 119
Reflecting on Resumés (Resumé Writing Practice) 120
Need for Information (Locating and Using Information) 121
Vocabulary Check-Up 122
News Words 123
Good Graphs for Good Grades 124–125
Preparing Today for Career Success Tomorrow 126–127
Timelines are Timeless (Organizing Information) 128
Who Said What? 129
Send a Letter (Letter Writing Practice) 130
Operation Observation 131
A Real-Life Application Using Estimation Skills 132–133
Science Savvy (Developing Familiarity with
   Science Methods and Process Skills) 134–135
Project Planning 136
Top Ten Tips for Preparing a Five-Star Report 137
Top Ten Test-Taking Tips 138

Chapter Four
Promoting Cooperative Learning and Group Interaction to Integrate School Success and Career Readiness 139

Cooperative Learning Overview 140-144
Team Learning 145
Money, Money, Money 146-148
Round Table 149
What are Your Values? (Recording Sheet) 150–158
Circle of Knowledge 159
Sample Prompts for Circle of Knowledge Activities 160
Jigsaw 161
Work Theories (Recording Sheet) 162–163
Think/Pair/Share 164
Think/Pair/Share Springboards For World of Work and Career Success 165
World of Work and Think/Pair/Share Recording Sheet 166
Three-Step Interview 167
The Three Economic and Societal Stages of Growth in Western Civilization 168–170
Fifteen Tools for Team Decision-Making and Problem-Solving 171–175
Ways to Improve Team Collaboration Skills for Problem Solving 176
Questions to Find Answers For
   When Observing a Team Meeting or Problem-Solving Session 177
Create a Co-Worker 178

    Imagination When it Comes to Business 179
    Learning in a Career Study Group 180
    Create a Television Commercial 181
    Role Models that Make a Difference 182
    Investigating Cooperative Learning 183–184

Chapter Five

Facilitating Authentic Assessment to Integrate School Success and Career Readiness **185**

    Facilitating Authentic Assessment 186–187
    Self-Analysis of My Readiness to be a Classroom Career Expert 188–189
    Questions Apt to Be Asked During a Job Interview 190
    Fast-Paced Changes in the Workplace (Product Assessment) 191
    The Workplace Collage 192
    School Success is No Accident (Suggestions for Success) 193–194
    Ten Possible Product Challenges 195
    Ten Product/Performance Projects 196
    Six Performances to Showcase What You Have Learned About Career Education 197
    Ten Career Book Projects to Create 198
    Suggested Journal Topics 199
    Communication Countdown 200
    Interviews are Important (Interview/Performance Assessment) 201
    Self-Help options for Looking at Career Clusters (Independent Project) 202
    Portfolio Rubric 203
    Rubric for Assessing the Quality of an Independent or Group Project,
        Product, or Performance 204
    The ABC's of What I've Learned About the World of Work 205–206

A Super-Practical Appendix to Integrate School Success and Career Readiness

    Job Fields to Consider 208
    Fourteen Suggestions for Parent Involvement
        In Helping Schools Prepare Tomorrow's Workers 209
    Planning a Career Day for Your School 210
    Conduct a Company Scavenger Hunt (Exploring Community Businesses) 211
    Competencies and Skills Identified in the SCANS Report 212–213
    Things to Think and Talk About 214
    Tasks to Try and Tell About 214
    Possible Reference Findings on Work/Career Topic 215–218

    Bibliography 219–221
    Index 222–223

PREFACE

Regardless of the role they play in the education of Middle Grades and High School students, today's educators are keenly aware of their responsibility to help prepare these citizens of tomorrow for their place in the world in which they will live and work. Realizing that each day the world of work is becoming increasingly complex, competitive, and demanding, educators know the importance of the schooling process as it influences a student's opportunities for career success.

Ever conscious of the fact that success in school is crucial to the development of a positive self-concept and an optimistic and enthusiastic outlook to the future, these educators are constantly looking for new and better ways to help all students achieve the optimum in school success. Research has proven that a positive learning community, attention to individual student needs, and the employment of student-centered, active learning strategies result in a higher number of student success stories.

Integrating School Success and Career Readiness has been written to present research-proven instructional strategies and organizational procedures in a clear and concise manner to meet the challenges faced daily by administrators, curriculum planners, teachers, and especially students. Each member of the school community often faces the school day with a feeling of "too much to do, too few tools, too little support, and too little time." It is, therefore, the authors' hope that the classroom-ready, student and teacher-friendly strategies, activities, projects, tools, and techniques in *Integrating School Success and Career Readiness* will help educators in their constant quest for means to afford a higher level of success for each student.

The content focus relevant to career awareness and school-to-work challenges has been integrated with emphasis on achievement of school success. This integration of content is intended to stimulate interest in and activate positive concern for both the immediate future and an introspective look at life-long goals. Additionally, basic skills essential to both school and career success have been built into the student activities in a boldly significant manner. Completion of these projects should result in increased readiness for both standardized tests and authentic assessment measures.

Each major section of the book includes:
- A comprehensive overview of a particular instructional focus
- Research findings specifically related to the focus
- List of key terms or concepts related to the focus

Chapter One: *Accommodating Differing Learning Styles, Abilities, and Interests to Integrate School Success and Career Readiness*

Read and Relate tasks, interest inventories, and checklists to integrate school success and career readiness

Guidelines for incorporating the Multiple Intelligences and learning stations into the preparation of high-quality lesson plans and student assignments are featured.

Chapter Two: *Developing Higher-Order Thinking Skills and Problem Solving Activities to Integrate School Success and Career Readiness*

Taxonomies, including Bloom's Taxonomy of higher-order thinking skills, Williams' Taxonomy of Creative Thought, and decision-making projects.

These cognitive taxonomies and exercises provide multiple foundations for infusing higher-order thinking skills into the educational process through the use of cognitive taxonomies, self-directed investigation cards, and calendars. The cognitive taxonomies offer useful foundations for the design of interdisciplinary units, student worksheets, learning stations, and group projects.

Chapter Three: *Using Basic Skills to Integrate School Success and Career Readiness*

Provides multiple avenues for presenting basic skills within a meaningful context of concept-rich content of high interest to the student. Opportunities for reinforcement of reading, writing, speaking, listening, math, social studies, and science skills and concepts are amply presented in lively fashion.

Chapter Four: *Promoting Cooperative Learning and Group Interaction to Integrate School Success and Career Readiness*

Presents valuable collaborative processes such as jigsaw, discussion groups, questionnaires, and projects.

Chapter Five: *Facilitating Authentic Assessment to Integrate School Success and Career Readiness*

Additional checklists, inventories, rating sheets, questionnaires, and summary sheets are provided to complement the assessment process.

A Super-Practical Appendix to Integrate School Success and Career Readiness

Supplies high-interest strategies, student activities and teacher tips for integrating school success and career readiness. Included are student outline and planning forms, topics for independent projects, creative writing aids, an annotated bibliography, and more. The comprehensive index will make it easy to keep track of this wealth of information.

This book was conceived and developed to aid those educators concerned with providing school success to beget career success for the students entrusted to their guidance. It is the authors' sincere hope that it will serve as a worthwhile reference and will afford support in helping to achieve this end.

CHAPTER ONE

ACCOMMODATING DIFFERING LEARNING STYLES, ABILITIES, AND INTERESTS TO INTEGRATE SCHOOL SUCCESS AND CAREER READINESS

Using Multiple Intelligences
   to Integrate School Success and Career Readiness.................................12–13
Multiple Intelligences and Career Chart..14–15
Multiple Intelligence Activities
   Exploring the World of Business..16–17
   Understanding Conflicts that Impact the World of Work.....................18–19
   Pondering Parental Support for Achievement.......................................20–21
   Extra! Extra! Careers in a Book...22–23
   Difficult Employees Can be Difficult to Work With..............................24–25
   Meeting the Needs of a Happy Employee...26–28
   Interdisciplinary Learning Stations 29–32
   What's Out There for Me?..33–34
   Using the Read and Relate Concept
      as an Instructional Tool..35
   Six Read and Relate Activities..36–38
Open-Ended Self-Evaluation Activities
   A One of a Kind, Unique You...39
   Occupations of Interest 40, 41
   Visualizing the Future..42, 43
   Job Preferences 44
   Personally Speaking..45
   Write and Reflect..46

Multiple Intelligences
Gardner's Theory

USING MULTIPLE INTELLIGENCES TO INTEGRATE SCHOOL SUCCESS AND CAREER READINESS

Dr. Howard Gardner's Theory of Multiple Intelligences is an interesting way to teach a concept or skill in any subject area. Dr. Gardner has identified eight multiple intelligences. He defines these intelligences as eight different types or ways of knowing, perceiving, and understanding the world around us. Gardner also makes it clear that one or two intelligences are often stronger and more developed in a person, although everyone has the capacity for nurturing all eight. It is important that teachers design lesson plans with these multiple intelligences in mind and that students practice using all eight of these intelligences in their work.

Howard Gardner's Theory of Multiple Intelligences provides teachers with an excellent model for the design of interdisciplinary units, student worksheets, learning stations, and group projects. Gardner is quick to point out that (1) every student has at least one dominant intelligence (although he or she may have more than one); (2) these intelligences can all be nurtured, strengthened, and taught over time; (3) the intelligences do not exist in isolation but interface and interact with one another when completing a task; and (4) the intelligences provide teachers with seven different ways to approach the curriculum. Gardner has identified and described eight major intelligences:

Verbal / Linguistic Dominance

Students strong in this type of intelligence have highly developed verbal skills, and often think in words. They do well on written assignments, enjoy reading, and are good at communicating and expressing themselves.

Logical/Mathematical

Students strong in this intelligence are able to think in abstractions and can handle complex concepts. They readily see patterns or relationships in ideas. They like to work with numbers and perform mathematical operations, and they approach problem-solving exercises with the tools of logic and rational thought.

VISUAL/SPATIAL Dominance

Students with this dominant intelligence think in images, symbols, colors, pictures, patterns, and shapes. They like to perform tasks that require "seeing with the mind's eye"—tasks that require them to visualize, imagine, pretend, or form images.

Body/Kinesthetic Dominance

Students dominant in this intelligence have strong body awareness and a sharp sense of physical movement. They communicate best through body language, physical gestures, hands-on activities, active demonstrations, and performance tasks.

Multiple Intelligences
Gardner's Theory

Musical/Rhythmic Dominance
Students with this dominant intelligence enjoy music, rhythmic patterns, variations in tones or rhythms, and sounds. They enjoy listening to music, composing music, interpreting music, performing to music, and learning with music playing in the background.

Interpersonal Dominance
Students with this dominant intelligence thrive on person-to-person interactions and team activities. They are sensitive to the feelings and needs of others and are skilled team members, discussion leaders, and peer mediators.

Intrapersonal Dominance
Students with this dominant intelligence prefer to work alone because they are self-reflective, self-motivated, and in tune with their own feelings, beliefs, strengths, and thought processes. They respond to intrinsic rather than extrinsic rewards and may demonstrate great wisdom and insight when presented with personal challenges and independent-study opportunities.

Naturalistic Dominance
Howard Gardner defines a naturalist as a person who recognizes flora and fauna plus other consequential distinctions in the natural world and uses the ability productively. A naturalist demonstrates the ability to understand patterns, relationships, and connections in nature.

The Theory of Multiple Intelligences can be used as a guide for the teacher who is interested in creating lesson plans that address one or more of the intelligences on a daily basis. Teachers should ask themselves the following questions when attempting to develop or evaluate classroom activities using the eight intelligences.

1. What tasks require students to write, speak, or read?
2. What tasks require students to engage in problem solving, logical thought, or calculations?
3. What tasks require students to create images or visual aids and to analyze colors, textures, forms, or shapes?
4. What tasks require students to employ body motions, manipulations, or hands-on approaches to learning?
5. What tasks require students to incorporate music, rhythm, pitch, tones, or environmental sounds in their work?
6. What tasks require students to work in groups and to interact with other students?
7. What tasks require students to express personal feelings, insights, beliefs, and self-disclosing ideas?
8. What tasks require students to identify people, plants, animals, and other features in our environments?

Multiple Intelligences and Career Chart

INTELLIGENCE	DESCRIPTION
Verbal/Linguistic	Intelligence of words and production of language
Logical/Mathematical	Intelligence of numbers, logic, and inductive reasoning
Visual/Spatial	Intelligence of pictures, mental images, and sight
Body/Kinesthetic	Intelligence of physical self, control of one's body movements, and learning by doing
Musical/Rhythmic	Intelligence of recognition and use of rhythmic or tonal patterns and sensitivity to sounds from the environment
Interpersonal	Intelligence of people skills, communication skills, and collaborative skills
Intrapersonal	Intelligence of the inner self, intuition, and emotions
Naturalistic	Intelligence of nature, environment, ecosystems, and one ruled by Mother Nature

STRATEGIES	CAREERS
Journal writing, making speeches, storytelling, reading	Novelists, comedians, journalists
Developing outlines, creating codes, calculating, problem solving	Accountants, lawyers, computer programmers
Drawing, using guided imagery, making mind maps, making charts	Architects, mechanical engineers, map makers
Role Playing, dancing, playing games, using manipulatives	Athletes, inventors, mechanics
Singing, performing, writing compositions, playing instruments, performing choral readings	Musicians, advertising designers, composers
Working with mentors and tutors, participating in interactive projects, using cooperative learning	Teachers, politicians, religious leaders
Using learning centers, participating in self-reflection tasks, using higher-order reasoning, taking personal inventories	Psychiatrists, counselors, entrepreneurs
Observing, digging, planting, displaying, sorting, uncovering, and relating	Conservationists, environmentalists, hikers, bird watchers

Multiple Intelligences Activity
Exploring Business

EXPLORING THE WORLD OF BUSINESS

Directions:

Work through these business-related activities to learn more about the exciting world of work and its many opportunities for students of tomorrow's workplace.

Verbal / Linguistic Intelligence

Write non-stop for five minutes discussing what you think are the three biggest problems facing businesses that use the Internet as a sales and marketing tool for their products and services.

Logical/Mathematical Intelligence

Plan a computer/technology/Internet-oriented business you would like to start as a "kid entrepreneur." List all of the capital resources you would need. Include tools, buildings, money, and all of the human resources you would need. Include employees and special skills, and all of the natural resources you would need. Include natural elements such as land, minerals, and raw materials.

VISUAL/SPATIAL Intelligence

Research to find out more about the trades that were necessary in the community life of Revolutionary War days long before technology came to be such an influence on the world. Construct a series of drawings showing the signs of these trades, such as silversmiths, innkeepers, cobblers, tailors, etc.

Multiple Intelligences Activity
Exploring Business

Bodily/Kinesthetic Intelligence

Pretend you are Bill Gates—the owner and chief stockholder of Microsoft. Act out a series of skits showing various reasons why you would hire and fire selected employees. Role-play both job interviewing and job firing episodes.

Musical/Rhythmic Intelligence

Investigate how computer-generated music is recorded and how various music companies use the Internet to promote their musical products. Locate and play some computer-generated musical compositions.

Interpersonal Intelligence

Stage a panel discussion of "charities" as business enterprises. Define "charity" and give examples of these organizations. Explain how they are financed, how they are organized, how they help people, and how they differ from other businesses. Finally, conduct a dialogue on how advanced technology has helped them to do their jobs more effectively.

Intrapersonal Intelligence

If you could meet the CEO (Chief Executive Officer) of any major company associated with advanced technological innovations, who would you like to spend the day with and what would you want to know and do?

Naturalistic Intelligence

Discover ways that technology and business have collaborated to deal with Mother Nature's disasters, such as those encountered through hurricanes, tornadoes, earthquakes, storms, floods, and other tragedies.

Multiple Intelligences Activity
Understanding Conflicts

UNDERSTANDING CONFLICTS THAT IMPACT THE WORLD OF WORK

Directions:

In the world of work, conflicts cause a great deal of anguish among and between employees and employers, producers and consumers, big business leaders and entrepreneurs, union members and non-union personnel, companies on the stock exchange and their stockholders, as well as national competitors and international competitors, just to name a few. Complete the following tasks as a means to understanding causes and kinds of conflict that are common in the workplace today.

Verbal / Linguistic Intelligence

Maintain a "conflict journal" for one week and record information about conflicts that you observe, learn about, or involve you. For each conflict situation:

1 Write down a brief description of the conflict.

2 Tell who is involved and what the conflict is about.

3 Explain how it started and how it escalated during the encounter.

4 Describe how each person felt about it and what each person wanted or needed out of it.

5 Record details on if and how it ended.

6 Define the type of conflict you thought it was.

Multiple Intelligences Activity
Understanding Conflicts

Logical/Mathematical Intelligence

Construct a chart that shows the following six ways of handling conflict: AGGRESSION, COLLABORATION, COMPROMISE, GIVE IN, AVOID OR DELAY, and APPEAL TO AUTHORITY. Write down some brief phrases and behaviors that are associated with each one. Also, write down some potential uses for each conflict along with some possible limitations.

VISUAL/SPATIAL Intelligence

Design a comic strip depicting a conflict situation that could arise between or among one of the groups suggested in the Verbal/Linguistic task above.

Bodily/Kinesthetic Intelligence

Create a role-play that acts out a possible conflict situation that could arise between or among one of the groups suggested in the Verbal/Linguistic task above.

Musical/Rhythmic Intelligence

Research to learn the process of producing a record. Discuss the conflicts that may result from differences in creative styles of the musicians, songwriters, record producers, etc.

Interpersonal Intelligence

Research to find out more information about the historical evolution of unions in corporate America and arrange a panel, a debate, or a group discussion to dialogue about the pros and cons of unions in the world of work today based on their economic and political history.

Intrapersonal Intelligence

Locate a newspaper or magazine article that focuses on some type of conflict that is occurring in the workplace. Cut out the article and write down some of your personal thoughts about and reactions to the conflict situation.

Naturalistic Intelligence

Investigate a conflict that has occurred or is occurring between groups of real estate and/or business developers and environmental or conservation groups in your community. Prepare a short report on the topic.

Multiple Intelligences Activity
Evaluating Importance of Parental Support

PONDERING PARENTAL SUPPORT FOR ACHIEVEMENT

Directions:

Verbal / Linguistic Intelligence

If you were a parent with a child your age, write down some of the rules you would make about: Homework, Extracurricular Activities, Grades, Friends, and Classroom Behavior.

Logical/Mathematical Intelligence

Assume the identity of one of your parents or guardians and write down how they would logically respond to each of these hypothetical questions: (1) How do you feel about your child's school achievement this year? (2) Has any subject or class been especially difficult for your child? (3) Has there been anything occurring lately that may be distracting your son/daughter from schoolwork?

VISUAL/SPATIAL Intelligence

Draw a picture to illustrate one or more of these positive coaching tips for parents: (1) Agree on and communicate expectations: (2) Let the learner struggle; (3) Connect effort with results; (4) Enforce academic time; (5) Use incentives; (6) Minimize anxiety; and (7) Use moderation.

Bodily/Kinesthetic Intelligence

Act out one of these scenarios depicting parenting pitfalls and how to avoid them in the home: (1) Unreasonable expectations; (2) The need to control; (3) Giving up; (4) Frequent use of payoffs; (5) Anger and guilt trips; (6) Panic; and (7) Punishment.

Multiple Intelligences Activity
Evaluating Importance of Parental Support

Musical/Rhythmic Intelligence

Determine what kinds of music you would allow your son or daughter to play while doing homework or studying for a test.

Interpersonal Intelligence

Set up a panel of students to discuss these characteristics of achievers for an audience of parents using personal stories and examples as part of the discussion (adding others of your own): (1) Achievers are goal-oriented; (2) Achievers are positive thinkers; (3) Achievers are confident; (4) Achievers are resilient; (5) Achievers have self-discipline; (6) Achievers have pride; (7) Achievers are proficient; and (8) Achievers are risk takers.

Intrapersonal Intelligence

Decide which of these profiles of underachievers' best fits you: (1) The Rebel who doesn't see the relevance of school; (2) The Conformist who has decided that doing well in school is just not worth it. (3) The Stressed Learner or the perfectionist who must always do it right; (4) The Struggling Student who doesn't know the basics of how to learn and manage time; (5) The Victim who is reluctant to accept responsibility for his/her lack of success; (6) The Distracted Learner who has personal problems or concerns that affect his/her school performance; (7) The Bored Student who truly needs more challenging activities due to advanced skills and abilities; (8) The Complacent Learner who settles for less than he/she is capable of; (9) The Single-Sided Achiever who has decided that only certain classes are worthy of concentrated attention and energy.

Naturalistic Intelligence

Mother Nature often enforces rules for both parents and their offspring as survival tactics in the out-of-doors. A large community in West Palm Beach, Florida, is now requiring parents to take an hour-long ethics course in how to behave on the sidelines while coaching or watching their children play in athletic league sports such as baseball and soccer. This is the first group in the nation to make sportsmanship training for parents a prerequisite to their child's participation. The program, which will cost $5 and be required for at least one parent or guardian per family, lays out the roles and responsibilities of a parent of a youth athlete in a 19-minute video and a handbook. Write a paragraph supporting or negating this practice from the point-of-view of a student, a parent or guardian, a coach, or a spectator.

Source: Adapted from: Heacox, D. (1991). Up From Under-Achievement. Minneapolis, MN: Free Spirit Publishing.

Multiple Intelligences Activity
Career Application

EXTRA! EXTRA! CAREERS IN A BOOK

Directions:

Verbal / Linguistic Intelligence

You are an editor for the book you have just read. In approximately 200 words or less, create a book jacket cover that will make someone really want to read this book. Re-telling important or interesting events in the story can do this.

Logical/Mathematical Intelligence

You are a writer for *Late Night with David Letterman*. Your job is to come up with a list of the Top 10 Interesting Facts about your book and why each fact is interesting. Remember to keep them short and to the point.

VISUAL/SPATIAL Intelligence

You are a tour guide. Create a map or set of artifacts that you could use to take others on a guided tour through the town/towns your book encompasses.

Bodily/Kinesthetic Intelligence

You are an actor. Become your favorite character in this book. Dress up like him or her, talk like him or her, and try to think like him or her. Be prepared to stand up in front of the class and field questions the class will have about the "new you." Make sure you answer them in character!

Multiple Intelligences Activity
Career Application

Musical/Rhythmic Intelligence

You are a poet. Create a song or a poem about your book. It could be something that could be a useful opening for the book. Be sure to convey how the book makes you feel.

Interpersonal Intelligence

You are an author! Working with a small group of peers, develop alternative endings to your book that include everyone's ideas. You start by explaining the synopsis of the story to them. Then each of you begins to write an ending. After five minutes of writing, you pass your paper to the left and continue writing on the paper you have just received. After your paper comes back to you, share the finished product with your group.

Intrapersonal Intelligence

You are a journalist. Imagine that you are the main character in this book. Write a series of journal entries that describe the feelings this character is going through. Directly to the right of these entries, write about how you felt when you read this particular passage. Check to see if you and the character seem to think similarly or differently.

Naturalistic Intelligence

You are a naturalist. Imagine that you have been asked to plan a unique outdoor field experience for the main characters in your book. Where would you go? What would you do? How would you record what you see?

Reviewing Causes of Multiple Intelligences Activity
Behavior Difficulties

DIFFICULT EMPLOYEES CAN BE DIFFICULT TO WORK WITH

Difficult employees are those who are unhappy in their work roles and "act out" their unhappiness by complaining, goofing off, stealing time, and sometimes being rude or disruptive to others. Very often these difficult employees are bright, intelligent, and creative people who can't seem to express themselves in more productive ways.

Directions:

Verbal / Linguistic Intelligence

Write a paragraph describing ways that difficult students act out their frustrations when they are unhappy in their schooling activities. Compare these to ways employees might react when unhappy in their work activities.

Logical/Mathematical Intelligence

Construct a list of "bad behaviors" that one might expect to see in a classroom setting that houses a large number of unhappy, unproductive, and underachieving students. Circle those that might also be displayed under similar circumstances in the workplace.

VISUAL/SPATIAL Intelligence

Create a mural of a king-size workplace divided into two large sections. Label one section "Difficult Employees" and another section "Satisfied Employees." Draw individuals "acting out" their negative and/or positive behaviors, portraying as many different situations as you can think of.

Reviewing Causes of Behavior Difficulties

Multiple Intelligences Activity

Bodily/Kinesthetic Intelligence

Create and act out a set of exaggerated scenarios depicting each of the following "difficult employee" relationships with their boss, subordinates, or peers:

1. Want to follow their own preference and refuse to be told what to do by their superiors.
2. Get bored with repetitious and uncreative work.
3. Become unproductive when not totally challenged.
4. Come in late and leave early.
5. Dislike working for their disorganized bosses or managers.
6. Resent working with poor tools, equipment, or conditions.
7. Want to have a say in what they do and how things turn out.
8. Insist on a variety of tasks.
9. Beg for more responsibility, authority, and choice.
10. Push to learn new skills.
11. Want to be recognized when they do good work.
12. Want to take a break and have some fun.

Musical/Rhythmic Intelligence

Select pieces of music (or lyrics of music) that you think best represent an environment of disharmony and unhappiness and/or that best represent an environment of harmony and happiness. Make these into a musical or lyrical collage.

Interpersonal Intelligence

Work with a small group of peers and analyze the list of exaggerated scenarios from the bodily/kinesthetic activity above. Decide which of the twelve situations are most likely to occur in traditional classroom settings and develop some possible solutions to make things better for both teacher and student alike.

Intrapersonal Intelligence

Review the list of exaggerated scenarios from the bodily/kinesthetic activity above and decide which of these situations would bring out the most frustration and unhappiness in you and why.

Naturalistic Intelligence

Research to find out what kinds of things are most likely to bring out the "killer instinct" of various members within a given animal species.

Multiple Intelligences Activity
Looking at Employees' Basic Needs

MEETING THE NEEDS OF A HAPPY EMPLOYEE

The well-known psychologist, Abraham Maslow, determined that all human beings have a set of common needs. He described these needs as: The need for survival, the need for security, the need for belonging, the need for prestige, and the need for fulfillment.

Through his studies, Maslow concluded that these needs occur in levels from the most basic to the most satisfying. His work further suggested that people of all walks of life spend their days seeking fulfillment of one or more of these needs. A pyramid chart is often used to portray the five levels of needs as identified by Maslow.

Maslow's Hierarchy of Needs shows that all humans have the same basic needs.

The five needs are:

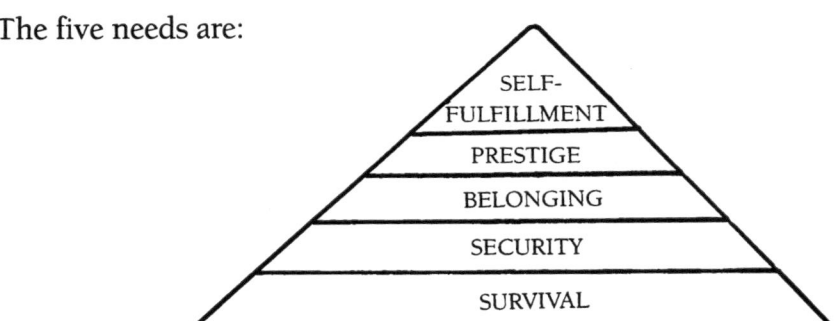

The Need to Survive: Our basic need is to survive. You might compare that to a cave man killing a rabbit and crawling into a cave to cook and eat it.

The Need for Security: The next need is security. The caveman may kill several rabbits, then roll a stone in front of the cave door to protect his assets.

The Need to Belong: Soon the caveman may feel lonely. Since he has enough rabbit for today and tomorrow, he invites some other cave people to share with him. He has now satisfied his need for belonging.

The Need for Prestige: Once he has others around, he appoints himself Chief. This satisfies his need for prestige.

The Need for Self-fulfillment: Finally, his group is secure enough to decorate the cave walls with paintings and dance and sing. He is praised for having made it all possible and has reached the level of self-fulfillment.

Multiple Intelligences Activity
Looking at Employees' Basic Needs

MEETING THE NEEDS OF A HAPPY EMPLOYEE

Directions:

Refer to the Maslow's Hierarchy of Needs (page 26) to complete this activity.

Verbal / Linguistic Intelligence

When one studies the field of economics, we talk about "needs" and "wants" of consumers. Explain the difference between the two and give examples of each.

Logical/Mathematical Intelligence

Develop a powerful argument and story to demonstrate that Maslow's Hierarchy of Needs is also applicable to the schooling process for students. They, too, have these needs that must be met as part of the educational process.

Visual/Spatial Intelligence

Reproduce a large version of Maslow's Ladder or Hierarchy of Needs and fill in words or phrases that you think best represent or reflect each.

Bodily/Kinesthetic Intelligence

Perform and/or create dramas to illustrate each of the five levels of need as identified by Maslow.

Musical/Rhythmic Intelligence

Pick out an instrument or a composition that you think best represents each level of Maslow's Hierarchy.

Multiple Intelligences Activity
Looking at Employees' Basic Needs

Interpersonal Intelligence
Use a human graph to see where each person in your advisory class stands on the ladder of needs as it relates to their personal situation.

Intrapersonal Intelligence
Evaluate your personal growth in terms of the five levels of needs and identify where you are at this point in time. Give reasons for your decision.

Naturalistic Intelligence
Offer a physical interpretation of how your body reacts to stress when one's needs at school, at home, at work, or at play are not being met at various levels on the ladder.

Reflection:

How can you see Maslow's Hierarchy of Basic Needs reflected in your thoughts about future career choices? How important is it to you to search for a career that would afford satisfaction of all of these needs? Is one more important to you than the others? What are the implications of this need in regard to the lifestyle you aspire to as an adult? Will it impose financial, geographical, or leisure time restraints on your career choice? Will the rewards outweigh the personal demands?

INTERDISCIPLINARY LEARNING STATIONS

Traditional classrooms are centered on rows of student desks lined up neatly in such a way that focus is on the teacher who is presenting a teacher-directed lesson. This "sage on the stage" image of the relationship between students and teachers is now being questioned and the image of "guide on the side" is more accurately describing today's interaction between students and teacher.

The interdisciplinary learning station is an alternative way of managing students and their diversity in learning styles and abilities. They promote individual time frames, enhance self-concept, and encourage student choice and independence. A learning station is an institutional display or collection of educational tasks that are presented in a manner that encourages the student to explore a topic, build a concept, or refine a skill. Likewise, a learning station is a vehicle through which kids learn how to learn, to think creatively and critically, to make choices, to plan, and to assess their progress. In short, the broad goals of learning stations are: (1) to motivate student learning; (2) to diagnose student learning experiences; (3) to prescribe necessary learning tasks; and (4) to enrich student learning experiences.

Interdisciplinary Learning Stations

The most successful learning station models are those that feature a theme and include interdisciplinary tasks throughout the stations. This integrated approach to subject matter helps students to build bridges between and among disciplines and to avoid fragmentation as they move from one topic, one classroom, or one teacher to another. In short, they are more likely to do better when learning is connected since the real work is integrated.

When designing learning stations, one should keep in mind the following steps:

1. Identify the interdisciplinary content areas to be addressed.

2. Identify the objectives within each of those content areas.

3. Determine which objectives to present through teacher-directed activities and which to present through stations.

4. Plan and construct stations.

5. Develop the skill or content objectives into learning activities that include both applying and extending tasks using Bloom and/or Williams' taxonomies as a model for infusing thinking skills throughout the stations.

6. Create a system for assigning stations and station activities that are multi-leveled.

7. Develop a record keeping system for stations as well as a process for students to use in recording their progress and/or reactions.

8. Structure a teacher-directed introduction to each learning station theme that outlines the purposes of each unit of study and discusses the learning tasks that will be included as part of each station. Also use this time to establish student rules or guidelines for working successfully in the learning station setting.

9. Finally, observe students as they work at stations and schedule regular student/teacher discussion sessions to evaluate both students' work habits with stations and the quality of the tasks that they perform in the stations.

Interdisciplinary Learning Stations

Learning stations can be organized around tables or clusters of desks, bulletin boards, wall posters/hangings, bookshelves, chalkboards, filing cabinets, portable screens to partition sections of the classroom, or scatter rugs around the room.

Interdisciplinary Learning Stations

One procedure for designing an interdisciplinary learning station theme that works well is the use of an interdisciplinary planning web. The web helps teachers create a learning map of multiple topics related to a single theme that could ultimately become the foundation for a series of learning experiences for inclusion within the learning station framework.

The web on the following page illustrates a learning station plan encompassing activities found in this book. Please note that while the plan is included as a model for use in developing additional learning stations appropriate to meet specific group needs, it is also ready for classroom use as a stand-alone learning station.

This plan is followed by a blank web design for you to use to design your own learning station. Topics for additional learning stations that might be developed using pages from the book include:

Money Matters:
Exploring the role money plays in career choices

Business Smarts:
Investigating the world of business and business structures

Cool School:
Looking at school success as it influences individual career options

At Least A Thousand Things to Do:
Finding out about the many career options available to today's workers

Employers and Employees:
Assessing the roles and interdependence of management and workers

People Need Each Other:
Exploring collaborative learning and work relationships

Looking to the Future:
Visualizing the work world of the future and the challenges faced by workers of tomorrow

Web Lesson Plan

WHAT'S OUT THERE FOR ME?

WHAT'S OUT THERE FOR ME?
Looking at the World of Work from a Personal Standpoint

1. Thinking About Jobs (pg. 82–83) Examining Job Options/William's Taxonomy Introduction and Motivation for study of personal interests and career options.

2. What's Your Interest? (pg. 52–53) Assessing Career Interest/Bloom's Taxonomy Critical and Creative Thinking Activity to examine interest areas.

3. Meeting the Needs of Happy Employees (pg. 27–28) Maslow's Hierarchy of Basic Needs/Multiple Intelligences Looking at needs and wants as related to the world of work.

4. Occupations of Interest (pg. 40–41) Personal Interest Survey/Open-Ended Creative Thinking Activity ranking categories of occupations according to personal interests.

5. Occupational Values (pg. 150–158) Round Table/Cooperative Learning Activity determining feelings related to values in the work place through collaborative investigation.

6. Narrowing Down Work Preferences (pg. 50–51) Personal Preferences/Bloom's Taxonomy focus on workplace preferences as determined by personal values.

7. Personally Speaking (pg. 45) Evaluating Personal Strengths/Product Assessment Activity Reflective thinking on the world of work.

8. Visualizing the Future (pg. 42–43) Summing up Interests/Creative Thinking Activity Assessment activity with ranking system and summary or vision of the future as reflected by personal goals.

Integrating School Success & Career Readiness
©2000 by Incentive Publications, Inc. Nashville, TN.

Web Lesson Plan

Build your own unit

INTERDISCIPLINARY LEARNING CENTER PLAN
FOR INTEGRATING SCHOOL SUCCESS AND CAREER READINESS

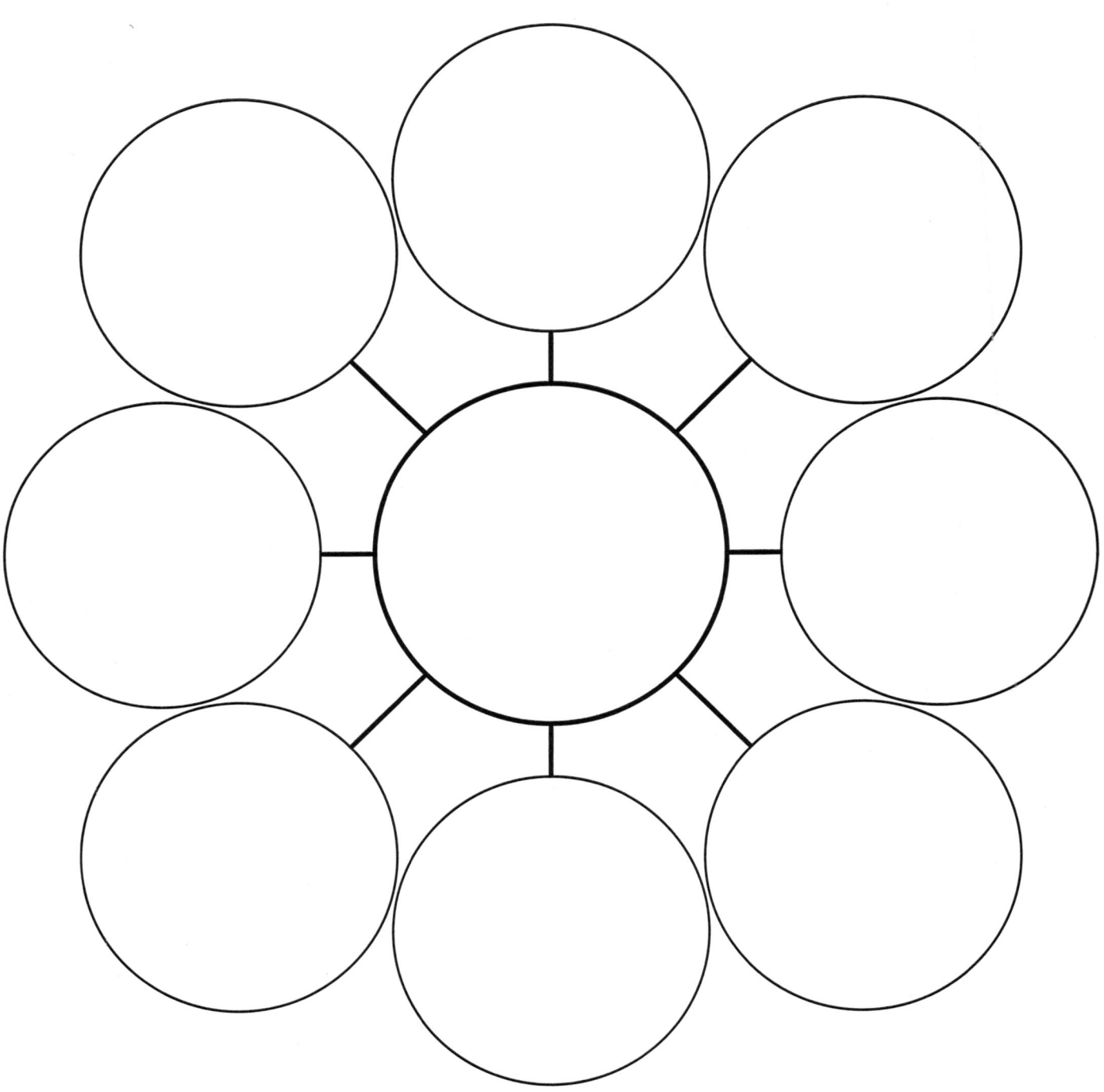

USING THE READ AND RELATE CONCEPT AS AN INSTRUCTIONAL TOOL

Read and Relate activities require the student to read or review a set of important concepts in a given subject area and then use these concepts as springboards for applying a range of creative or critical thinking skills.

Using the textbook or a favorite set of alternative reference materials, the teacher begins the Read and Relate process by selecting a number of ideas related to the topic that is being taught as part of an instructional unit. These ideas should be representative of key facts that the student should learn. It is crucial that these ideas lend themselves easily to a number of extended reading, writing, or thinking exercises that can provide opportunities for students to apply the facts in a new and different context.

Once the teacher has generated a list, the concepts are written as a series of short, descriptive paragraphs to be reviewed by the student. The paragraphs should be approximately three to five sentences in length, and they should be presented in a logical or sequential manner.

Next, teachers should use Bloom's Taxonomy, William's taxonomy, or any of Gardner's Multiple Intelligences as a basis for developing a follow-up reading, writing, speaking, or thinking activity for each factual paragraph. The activity should require the student to "do something" with the concept in a new and different way. The intent of this instructional strategy is to help the student understand that many important ideas learned in one subject area can be related to ideas in another subject area.

Notice how each descriptive paragraph is followed by a special application challenge for students to complete.

Read and Relate Activity

PERCEPTIONS OF WORK

WORK-RELATED QUOTATIONS

READ.
"I don't pity any man who does hard work worth doing. I admire him. I pity the creature who does not work, at whichever end of the social scale he may regard himself as being."
– Theodore Roosevelt, in a speech in Chattanooga, Tennessee, September 8, 1902.

"Employment gives health, sobriety, and morals. Constant employment and well-paid labor produces, in a country like ours, general prosperity, content, and cheerfulness."
– Daniel Webster, in a speech in the U.S. Senate, July 25, 1846.

RELATE.
Many famous business and world leaders have talked about their views on work and labor over the years. Write down your reactions to each of the above quotations by Roosevelt and Webster and comment on your perceptions of work and labor as a young person in this new century.

FINDING A BETTER WAY

TIME AND TASKS

READ.
A major contribution that employees can make in their workplace setting involves taking the initiative to look for ways to improve the work processes, products, services, and systems that are a vital part of how the organization does business. Some ways to analyze tasks associated with most jobs are:

(1) Imagine you were doing the task for the first time. Would you do it the way you are doing it now?
(2) If you had to, how could you do the task twice as fast? Five times as fast? Ten times as fast?
(3) What would be a completely different way of doing a task? and
(4) Do you really need to do the task? What would happen if you skipped it?

RELATE.
Think of a task that you commonly perform as a worker or helper at home or at school. Apply each of the four suggestions listed above to analyze the task, and if possible, improve its efficiency or its effectiveness.

Read and Relate Activity

AN INTERESTING PHENOMENON
PART-TIME JOBS

READ.
Several major studies have been done over the years on the short and long-term value of part-time jobs for teens. Did you know that: (1) High school students who work part-time usually make more money later in life than students who don't work during school; and (2) High school seniors who work 20 hours per week are expected to earn 20 percent more after college or university than those who don't work during high school; and (3) Most students who work up to 20 hours per week actually have better grades than those who don't work at all. The bottom line is that part-time jobs can ease one's transition into the workplace because these jobs will help a person improve their knowledge of the job market, gain some workplace skills, and make valuable contacts.

RELATE.
Create a banner, billboard, or advertisement that promotes part-time jobs for high school students highlighting both the positive benefits of these work experiences along with some cautions to be considered.

LISTEN UP!
LISTENING SKILLS

READ.
An employee spends most of his/her working day communicating with others—through telephone conversations, service to customers, dialogue with co-workers, and exchanges with a boss or supervisor. One's ability to communicate through reading, writing, speaking, and listening influences one's job success since only the knowledge of the job is more important than communication skills as a predictor of success. The average worker spends 55% of his/her time listening and only 23% of his/her time speaking on any given day.

RELATE.
Work with a partner and complete each of these "listening activities" several times throughout the week or month to improve your listening skills.

ACTIVITY ONE: Sit back-to-back with a partner and select a sample object or design for each of you to draw without seeing it as you carefully listen to his or her specific directions on what to do. Compare final products with the original item.

ACTIVITY TWO: Ask a partner to dictate a sentence of 20 or so words, reading it aloud only three times at first. Write the sentence from memory and compare it with the original. Can you get to the point where it needs to be read only one or two times?

ACTIVITY THREE: Ask a partner to list ten unrelated items found at her home, at school, at the mall, or in some other location for you to remember in sequence. As the words are called, listen carefully and then, after one minute, repeat the list in the exact order as dictated.

Integrating School Success & Career Readiness
©2000 by Incentive Publications, Inc. Nashville, TN.

Read and Relate Activity

SO MANY CHOICES
CAREERS

READ.
When studying careers, it is important to teach students a realistic view of available career options. There are thousands of career choices available today and with each technological advance and each major change in society, new careers are emerging as others are diminishing. In fact, most of the jobs that middle schoolers will qualify for in the future have not yet been invented. Less than half the workforce in the industrial world will be holding conventional full-timers. Insiders will be the new minority and every year more and more people will be self-employed. There are many ways of dividing these careers into categories or clusters for easy reference or access.

RELATE.
Make a list of at least 100 occupations that you can think of and write them in alphabetical order. Next, regroup these occupations in at least five different clusters or categories stating the criteria used for each classification structure.

DRIVERS OF CHANGE
CHANGE

READ.
There are three major forces of change that are reshaping our world and the way we live. The first of these is people. As the world population continues to grow, many people compete for scarce resources and generate new ideas. The second major force is technology. Well over 80% of the world's technological advances have occurred since 1900 and with more people to come, a rapidly accelerating rate of technological change is guaranteed. The third powerful force driving change is information or knowledge. The amount of information available in the world is doubling every three to five years. Far more knowledge, reaching far more people, far faster than ever before leads to a better informed population—which means better chances for change.

RELATE.
Draw a series of editorial cartoons depicting each of the three driving forces of change using the principles of exaggeration, humor, and graphics to get your points across. If you can think of other change factors, add these to your drawings as well.

Creative Thinking Activity
Art

A ONE OF A KIND, UNIQUE YOU

Directions:

Every person is a one-of-a-kind unique human being. Understanding your talents, abilities, likes, dislikes, strengths, and weaknesses will help you to set realistic goals and objectives leading to school success.

Design your own personal coat of arms based on seriously thought out and carefully-defined self-understanding. Decorate your coat of arms with words, phrases, drawings, and symbols that describe the "one-of-a-kind, unique you." Be sure to feature your special strengths, talents, and interests that help you to achieve school success. Looking to the future, add the unique abilities that you are nurturing now to help you become successful as a member of the future work force.

Open-Ended Creative Thinking Activity
Personal Interest Survey

OCCUPATIONS OF INTEREST

Directions:

Rank order this list of sixteen categories of occupations according to which have the most appeal to you and which have the least appeal to you. Give reasons for your first three and last three choices.

____ Executive, administrative, and managerial occupations

____ Engineers, scientists, and related occupations

____ Social science, social service, and related occupations

____ Teachers, librarians, and counselors

____ Health-related occupations

____ Writers, artists, and entertainers

____ Technologists and technicians

____ Marketing and sales occupations

____ Administrative support occupations, including clerical

____ Service occupations

____ Agricultural and forestry occupations

____ Mechanics and repairers

____ Construction occupations

____ Production occupations

____ Transportation and material moving occupations

____ Handlers, equipment cleaners, helpers, and laborers

Open-Ended Creative Thinking Activity
Personal Interest Survey

The occupations that are of the most interest to me at the present time are:

1. _____ ,

2. _____ , and

3. _____

because _____

_____

_____

_____

_____

_____

_____

The occupations that are of least interest to me at the present time are:

14. _____ ,

15. _____ , and

16. _____

because _____

_____

_____

_____

_____

_____

_____

Creative Thinking Activity
Summing Up Interests

VISUALIZING THE FUTURE

Directions:

Visualizing allows one to imagine, reach beyond reality, wonder, expand on the present, and dream of the future. Langston Hughes, a famous poet, wrote,

> "Hold fast to your dreams, because without dreams
> man is as a bird with a broken wing."

Visualizing the future will enable you to dream of places you want to go and things you want to achieve as an adult. As you visualize the life you want to be living ten years from now, there are some things you can do now to help yourself achieve this vision of the future. Pondering the following issues may help you on the way to realizing your dreams.

After reading and reflecting on each starter statement, quickly write your spontaneous response to complete and expand on each sentence.

1. As an adult, I would really like to _____.
2. A career that would help me to achieve this goal would be _____.
3. In order to be successful in this career, I would need to be good at _____ _____.
4. To learn more about this career I could _____ _____.
5. Some things I could do now to help prepare for this career are _____ _____.
6. The thing I would like most about this career is _____ _____.
7. Something I might not like about this career is _____ _____.
8. When I look ahead to my life as an adult I _____ _____.

Reflect on and review your completed statements. Use understandings gained to complete the accompanying rating sheet and reflective summary.

Creative Thinking Activity
Summing Up Interests

To help you better understand your own personal feelings about the future in terms of their importance to you, rank the following from 1 to 12. A score of one is the most important and a score of 12 is the least in importance. When you have finished, use the space at the bottom of the page to write a paragraph summarizing your vision of the future as reflected by your goals.

1. Money
2. Fame
3. Free time
4. Fortune
5. Helping others
6. Excitement
7. Learning new things
8. Team work
9. Low stress
10. Challenging tasks
11. Pleasant surroundings
12. Positive reinforcement

SUMMARY:

_____
_____
_____
_____
_____
_____
_____
_____
_____
_____
_____
_____
_____
_____

Creative Thinking Activity
Assessing Personal Preferences

JOB PREFERENCES

My Special Skills With People

My Special Skills With Things

My Special Skills With Knowledge

Desired Working Conditions

Desired Level of Position & Salary

Desired Level of Education Required

Desired Kinds & Backgrounds of Co-Workers

Geographic Preferences

Preferred Work Hours/ Arrangements

Other

Reflective Summary of the Perfect Job For Me

Complete the building outline above by filling in the WINDOWS OF INFORMATION found on each floor, and when considered all together, outline the ideal job for you at this point in your life. Complete this BUILDING OF JOBS every few months to assess whether your feelings and beliefs about the world of work are changing as you grow and mature.

Creative Thinking Activity
Evaluating Personal Strengths

PERSONALLY SPEAKING

Directions:

It is critical that individuals at the middle and high school levels leave each grade with a positive sense of self and an understanding of what personal qualities serve them best. Complete one or more of the suggested activities below to help you clarify your personal strengths.

1. Free-write for approximately ten minutes, bragging about the things that you do well. Then use this information to create an advertisement, poster, or collage promoting "you at your best."

2. Prepare a collection of quotes that inspire, motivate, challenge, or stimulate you to achieve. Print these on long strips of paper or oak tag and keep them visible at all times.

3. Create a "Terrific Me" folder that contains all types of artifacts that represent you at your best. These can include school papers or projects, personal notes or greeting cards, awards, programs of participation, report cards, announcements, or journal entries.

4. Prepare an "autograph book" and circulate it among your peers and teachers. Ask them to write something nice and special about you from their perspective on a page in the book.

5. Interview both a peer and an adult whom you admire and whom you respect. Ask each individual to share with you some of the observations and reflections about your personal qualities. Tape-record their responses and play them back from time to time.

6. Go back over your life and create a timeline of accomplishments. Try to record an event, accolade, tribute, learned skill, or growth experience (good or bad) for each year of your life to date.

7. Prepare an "autograph book" and circulate it among your peers and Keep a learning log with entries every day for a month. Write down what good things happen to you, are said about you, or impressions and observations that might benefit you. Review these at the end of the month and try to draw some conclusions about how they illustrate your personal qualities, aptitudes, and talents.

Creative Thinking Activity
Journal Topics

WRITE AND REFLECT

Directions:

Keeping a daily journal will help you record and reflect on happenings in your daily life and gain a better understanding of yourself and the world in which you live.

Select one of the starter statements below to use as a springboard to a journal entry related to school success.

1. The class I have the most trouble with is . . .

2. I wish teachers in our school would finally . . .

3. Standardized tests as a means of measuring student achievement are . . .

4. One thing that I really like about school this year . . .

5. I wish I were better at . . .

6. Something that made me very uncomfortable . . .

7. My study skills are . . .

8. My classes this year as compared to my classes last year . . .

9. The grading system in our school . . .

10. Students of my generation wish our parents . . .

11. The perfect school day for me . . .

12. I think advances in the use of technology will make learning for students of my age . . .

13. Our school advisory program . . .

14. One thing that I could do to improve my grades . . .

CHAPTER TWO

DEVELOPING HIGHER-ORDER THINKING SKILLS AND PROBLEM-SOLVING ABILITIES TO INTEGRATE SCHOOL SUCCESS AND CAREER READINESS

    Using Bloom's Taxonomy to Integrate School Success and Career Readiness 48–49
    Narrowing Work Preferences (Bloom's Taxonomy Activity) 50–51
    What's Your Interest? (Assessing Career Interests/Bloom's Activity) 52–53
    Digging into the Dictionary (Improving Dictionary Skills) 54–56
    Money Matters (Money Management/Bloom's Activity) 57–58
    Business Smarts (Business Structures/Bloom's Activity) 59–60
    Finding Out About Your State's Economy
        (Analyzing State Economy/Bloom's Activity).. 61–62
    Defining and Diffusing Conflict (Conflict Resolution/Bloom's Activity) 63–64
    Investigation Cards 65–66
    Investigating the World of Work 67–69
    Business in the News 70–71
    Using Williams' Taxonomy to Integrate School Success and Career Readiness ... 72–73
    How's Your Performance? 74–75
    Creating a Climate for Learning 76–77
    Looking at Technology 78–79
    Technology in the Workplace 80–81
    Thinking About Jobs 82–83
    Confronting Conflict 84–85
    School Safety and Student Security 86–87

    Creative Thinking Exercises
        What's Your Opinion? 88
        Using Krathwohl's Taxonomy to Explore Gender Issues 89
        Quality Counts 90
        Reflecting on Grades 91–92
        Searching for Feelings 93
        Decisions, Decisions 94–95
        Goals to Go 96–97
        Lists that Inspire Creative Thinking 98–99
        21st Century Career Challenges and Choices to Consider 100–101
        Exploring Creative-Thinking Challenges Related to School Success 102
        Two Sides of Every Career 103
        Eliminating the Negatives Related to School Success 104–105
        Eliminating the Negative Sack 106

Bloom's Taxonomy

USING BLOOM'S TAXONOMY TO INTEGRATE SCHOOL SUCCESS AND CAREER READINESS

Bloom's Taxonomy is a well-known model for teaching critical thinking skills in any subject area. Based on the work of Benjamin Bloom, the taxonomy consists of six different thinking levels arranged in a hierarchy of difficulty.

Any student can function at each level of the taxonomy provided the content is appropriate for his or her reading ability. In order for teachers to consistently design lesson plans that incorporate all six levels, they should use the taxonomy to structure all student objectives, all information sessions, all questions, all assigned tasks, and all items on tests.

On the opposite page is a brief summary of the six taxonomy levels with a list of common student behaviors, presented as action verbs, associated with each level. When developing learning tasks and activities around Bloom's Taxonomy, it is important to include in each set at least one activity for each level of the taxonomy. Keep a copy of the Bloom's page in your lesson-planning book so it will be handy when you need it.

Bloom's Taxonomy can be used to structure sets of learning tasks, student worksheets, cooperative learning group assignments, and independent study units. The following topics were selected to be of high appeal to students. These topics will further their interest and desire for both school success and the world of work.

BLOOM'S TAXONOMY OF CRITICAL THOUGHT

KNOWLEDGE

Learn the information.
Sample Verbs: Define, find, follow directions, identify, know, label, list, memorize, name, quote, read, recall, recite, recognize, select, state, and write.

COMPREHENSION

Understand the information.
Sample Verbs: Account for, explain, express in other terms, give examples, give in own words, group, illustrate, infer, interpret, paraphrase, recognize, re-tell, show, simplify, summarize, and translate.

APPLICATION

Use the information.
Sample Verbs: Apply, compute, construct, convert (in math), demonstrate, derive, develop, discuss, generalize, interview, investigate, keep records, model, participate, perform, plan, produce, prove (in math), solve, use, utilize.

EVALUATION

Judge the information.
Sample Verbs: Assess, defend, evaluate, grade, judge, measure, perform a critique, rank, recommend, select, test, validate, verify.

ANALYSIS

Break the information down into its component parts.
Sample Verbs: Analyze, compare, contrast, criticize, debate, determine, diagram, differentiate, discover, draw conclusions, examine, infer, relate, search, sort, survey, take apart, uncover.

SYNTHESIS

Put information together in new and different ways.
Sample Verbs: Build, combine, create, design, imagine, invent, make up, present, produce, and propose.

Personal Preferences Activity
Bloom's Taxonomy

NARROWING WORK PREFERENCES

According to selected experts, there are several methods for narrowing down one's work preferences. Perhaps the most challenging of these options is to focus on the process of identifying work values. These values are outlined here for you to consider:

Adventure:	working in a job that requires taking risks.
Authority:	working in a job in which you use your position to control others.
Competition:	working in a job in which you compete with others.
Creativity And Self-Expression:	working in a job in which you use your imagination to find new ways to do or say something.
Flexible Work Schedule:	working in a job in which you choose your hours to work.
Helping Others:	working in a job in which you provide direct services to persons with problems.
High Salary:	working in a job where many workers earn a large amount of money.
Independence:	working in a job in which you decide for yourself what work to do and how to do it.
Influencing Others:	working in a job in which you influence the opinions of others or decisions of others.
Intellectual Stimulation:	working in a job that requires a great amount of thought and reasoning.
Leadership:	working in a job for which you direct, manage, or supervise the activities of others.
Outside Work:	working out-of-doors.
Persuading:	working in a job in which you personally convince others to take certain actions.
Physical Work:	working in a job that requires substantial physical activity.
Prestige:	working in a job that gives you status and respect in the community.
Public Attention:	working in a job in which you attract immediate notice because of appearance or activity.
Public Contact:	working in a job in which you have day-to-day dealings with the public.
Recognition:	working in a job in which you gain public notice.
Work With Hands:	working in a job in which you use your hands or hand tools.
Work With Machines or Equipment:	working in a job in which you use machines or equipment.
Work With Numbers:	working in a job in which you use mathematics or statistics.

Personal Preferences Activity
Bloom's Taxonomy

KNOWLEDGE
Define "work values" as it relates to use in this workplace context.

COMPREHENSION
Write down three to five different occupations that could be associated with each of the work values.

APPLICATION
Prepare an interest inventory of five questions that could be used to survey a student's potential for any of the work values listed here.

EVALUATION
Divide a piece of paper into three columns. In the first column, list the work values that appeal to you the most. In the second column, list the work values that appeal to you the least. In the third column, list the work values that you are unsure about in terms of their appeal to you. Be able to justify your choices in both the first and second columns.

ANALYSIS
Determine which of the work values seems most technical, seems most influential, seems most important, and seems most social.

SYNTHESIS
Compose a classified ad for a local newspaper that promotes job opportunities in one or more of the work values.

Integrating School Success & Career Readiness
©2000 by Incentive Publications, Inc. Nashville, TN.

Assessing Career Interests Activity
Bloom's Taxonomy

WHAT'S YOUR INTEREST?

Description:

All jobs in the United States can be classified into twelve (12) different interest areas. These twelve areas are:

Artistic:	an interest in creative expression of feelings or ideas.
Scientific:	an interest in discovering, collecting, and analyzing information about the natural world and in applying scientific research findings to problems in medicine, the life sciences, and the nature sciences.
Plants and Animals:	an interest in working with plants and animals, usually outdoors.
Protective:	an interest in using authority to protect people and property.
Mechanical:	an interest in applying mechanical principles to practical situations by using machines or hand tools.
Industrial:	an interest in repetitive, concrete, organized activities done in a factory setting.
Business Detail:	an interest in organized, clearly defined activities requiring accuracy and attention to details, primarily in an office setting.
Selling:	an interest in bringing others to a particular point of view by using personal persuasion as well as sales and promotional techniques.
Accommodating:	an interest in catering to the wishes and needs of others, usually on a one-to-one basis.
Humanitarian:	an interest in helping others with their mental, spiritual, social, physical, or vocational needs.
Leading and Influencing:	an interest in leading and influencing others by using high-level verbal or numerical abilities.
Physical Performing:	an interest in physical activities performed before an audience.

Assessing Career Interests Activity
Bloom's Taxonomy

KNOWLEDGE

Define "interest areas" as it relates to use in this workplace context.

COMPREHENSION

Write down three to five different occupations that could be associated with each of the interest areas.

APPLICATION

Prepare an interest inventory of five questions that could be used to survey a student's potential for any of the interest areas listed here.

EVALUATION

Divide a piece of paper into three columns. In the first column, list the interest areas that appeal to you the most. In the second column, list the interest areas that appeal to you the least. In the third column, list the interest areas that you are unsure about in terms of their appeal to you. Be able to justify your choices in both the first and second columns.

ANALYSIS

Determine which of the interest areas seems most technical, seems most influential, seems most important, and seems most social.

SYNTHESIS

Compose a classified ad for a local newspaper that promotes job opportunities in one or more of the interest areas.

Dictionary Skills Activity
Bloom's Taxonomy

DIGGING INTO THE DICTIONARY

It has been said, "Now that we live in the information generation, knowing where to find the information you need when you need it is more important than knowing the information." The dictionary remains a primary source for locating information needed on a daily basis. Acquiring and using dictionary skills is still an important factor in school success. Complete the following set of activities to evaluate and improve your use of the dictionary as an important study aid.

KNOWLEDGE
List ten different types of information that can be found in dictionaries more quickly and efficiently than in other resources.

COMPREHENSION
Complete the Digging into the Dictionary Worksheet on the following page.

APPLICATION
Use your dictionary to locate three different pieces of information about a subject of interest to you. Summarize and rewrite the information in your own words.

EVALUATION
Write a brief paragraph explaining the components and organization of a new dictionary you would design for use by students of your age.

ANALYSIS
Compare and contrast the use of, and value to students of, a dictionary and a thesaurus. If you could have only one available for use during the completion of a social studies project, which one would you choose?

SYNTHESIS
Create a picture dictionary of at least fifteen words related to one of the following topics:
World Geography
The Solar System
Musical Instruments
Oceanography
Geometry
Poetry
Include more than one piece of information and an illustration for each word entry.

Dictionary Skills Activity
Bloom's Taxonomy

Reflection:

1 Tell how a dictionary would aid you in completing one of the following projects:

    1. Developing a science fair project

    2. Writing a book report or term paper

    3. Creating a word find or crossword puzzle

    4. Preparing a speech

    5. Writing poetry

2 Why is it important for tomorrow's work force to be able to locate and use information quickly and easily? Ponder this thought: what other sources of information are available to supplement, or in some instances replace, the dictionary as a primary source of word knowledge?

Dictionary Skills Activity
Bloom's Taxonomy

DICTIONARY PRACTICE WORKSHEET:

For a little practice in dictionary usage: Complete each blank in Column A with a word that begins with the given letter or letters, and is the appropriate part of speech. When you have finished Column A, rearrange the words in alphabetical order in Column B. Then write a synonym opposite each word in Column C.

Column A (Be sure each word is spelled correctly and is the appropriate part of speech.)	Column B (Be sure this column lists words in ABC order.)	Column C (Choose a good synonym for each word in Column B and write it in this column.)
sn _____ (noun)	_____	_____
el _____ (adjective)	_____	_____
ba _____ (noun)	_____	_____
qu _____ (adverb)	_____	_____
cr _____ (noun)	_____	_____
tr _____ (verb)	_____	_____
sl _____ (verb)	_____	_____
to _____ (noun)	_____	_____
le _____ (noun)	_____	_____
zo _____ (noun)	_____	_____
ea _____ (adjective)	_____	_____
an _____ (adverb)	_____	_____
th _____ (noun)	_____	_____
t_ _____ (verb)	_____	_____
dr _____ (adjective)	_____	_____
sl _____ (adverb)	_____	_____
m _____ (verb)	_____	_____
str _____ (verb)	_____	_____
bl _____ (adjective)	_____	_____
vel _____ (adjective)	_____	_____

Bloom's Taxonomy Activity
Money Management

MONEY MATTERS

Description:

One of the key ways to learn more about the world of work is to develop an appreciation for earning and spending one's own money before you are responsible enough to earn and spend somebody else's money. You might be interested to know that kids between the ages of 4 and 14 get most of their money from four sources, in this priority order: allowances, chores around the house, earning outside the home, and gifts. Interestingly, kids like to spend their money in these ways, again listed in priority order: savings accounts, junk food, toys and games, movies/shows/concerts/sports events, clothing, arcade video games, and miscellaneous items such as compact discs, cosmetics, jewelry, telephones, and other living expenses.

KNOWLEDGE
Use the dictionary to define the concept of "allowance" as used in this context.

COMPREHENSION
Write a paragraph, summarizing the multiple ways that you earn and spend money.

APPLICATION
Survey students in your advisory class to determine the average dollar amount earned per week by the total number of students who receive an allowance as well as the most common things they have to do to earn it.

EVALUATION
Justify saving at least half of everything you earn or receive as gifts.

ANALYSIS
Compare and contrast the earning and spending habits of today's teenager with that of your parents or guardians. How are they alike and how are they different?

SYNTHESIS
Design a campaign to raise the allowance average of students in your class. Publicize these issues: Why should you get a raise? How much should it be? What will you do to earn it? How will you spend it?

Integrating School Success & Career Readiness
©2000 by Incentive Publications, Inc. Nashville, TN.

Bloom's Taxonomy Activity
Money Management

Reflection:

Do you think money is an important factor to be considered when thinking about career choices for the future? Write a paragraph below to answer this important question. Then, rank the following in order of their importance to you, as you consider occupations to pursue as an adult: job satisfaction, environment, time required to prepare for entry level position, salary, opportunity for continued education, and/or on-the-job training.

_____

_____

_____

_____

_____

_____

_____

_____

_____

_____

_____

_____

_____

_____

Bloom's Taxonomy Activity
Business Structure

BUSINESS SMARTS

To learn more about the structure and innerworkings of a business, complete each of the following tasks.

KNOWLEDGE

Use a dictionary to define the following business-related concepts: boycott, budget, capital, consumer, entrepreneur, expenses, free enterprise system, income, interest, labor, lease, loan, market, producer, profit, raw materials, rent, retail.

COMPREHENSION

In your own words, explain what is involved in each of the following steps to plan, run, and evaluate a business plan for producing a simple toy product within your advisory class.

Step 1: Conducting market research to determine what types of toys are best for this purpose.

Step 2: Deciding on a business name and business partners.

Step 3: Determining what toy product is best to produce and at what retail price.

Step 4: Planning for equipment and raw materials for producing the product.

Step 5: Starting a bookkeeping process to record all expenses and income as they are incurred.

Step 6: Planning an advertising campaign and creating the advertisements.

Step 7: Producing the toy product in sufficient quantities.

Step 8: Establishing a retail space and selling the product.

Step 9: Settling the debts and figuring the profit.

Step 10: Evaluating the decisions made in Steps 1 through 9 and making suggestions for improvement or change if one were to do it again.

APPLICATION

Visit a local toy store to conduct your market research on various toys that are for sale. Consider various types of toys, prices of toys, quality of toys, recommended ages for the toys, and raw materials/skills required for producing the toys. Record your findings.

Integrating School Success & Career Readiness
©2000 by Incentive Publications, Inc. Nashville, TN.

Bloom's Taxonomy Activity
Business Structure

ANALYSIS

Write down a list of toy categories that could be potential products for you to sell as part of a Toy Marketplace for your advisory classroom. Be sure to include the pros and cons for producing each toy item. Consider puzzles, games, puppets, dolls, storybooks or coloring books, paper dolls and clothes, art kits, etc. Decide on a product to produce and a production and retail price for the construction and sale of the product, as well as multiple reasons for your final product choice.

EVALUATION

Prepare a ledger sheet that records all costs and expenses for this toy venture as well as any revenues and profits that were generated. Assess the toy marketplace activity in terms of its success, taking into account everything from time and energy spent on the project to profit margins on the sale of the product.

SYNTHESIS

Create a comprehensive toy development or production plan that includes information and timelines for making and selling the toy product. What special features will the toy have? What are the plans for getting materials and tools to make the toy? What steps will be taken to produce the toy? How will the labor be divided among the business partners? Where, when, and how will the toy be advertised and sold? If time permits, create a Toy Catalog that contains descriptions and prices for all of the toys produced in the advisory classroom for the Marketplace.

Reflection:

1. How does studying the structure of one specific business help you to understand other businesses? Name three other types of businesses that you would like to learn more about.

2. Compare and contrast the needs, challenges, and opportunities for profit of these businesses:
   a. An automobile manufacturing company and a retail automobile distributorship
   b. A dairy farm and an ice cream manufacturer
   c. A fabric designer and an up scale dress shop

Bloom's Taxonomy Activity
Analyzing State Economy

FINDING OUT ABOUT YOUR STATE'S ECONOMY

KNOWLEDGE

1. List three different sources you could use to find information about your state.
2. Record at least five different types of information about your state you can find in a newspaper.
3. Write a brief paragraph summarizing the types of information about your state that you can acquire from the Internet.
4. Name the three geographic areas of your state that offer the largest number of jobs.

COMPREHENSION

1. Explain the importance of the highway system to the economy of your state.
2. Outline a report you would write on the topic, "Major Industries of My State."

APPLICATION

1. Locate all the major rivers on a map of your state.
2. Produce a picture dictionary of forest and field animals native to your state.
3. Make an annotated listing of summer job opportunities readily available to high school students in your state.

Integrating School Success & Career Readiness
©2000 by Incentive Publications, Inc. Nashville, TN.

Bloom's Taxonomy Activity
Analyzing State Economy

ANALYSIS

1. Examine the early history of your state to find out how work opportunities influenced the location of the major cities or towns.
2. Compare and contrast the importance of an atlas and an encyclopedia to the study of tourist attractions offered by your state.
3. Determine why some parts of your state are less populated than others.

EVALUATION

1. Imagine how life in your state would be different today if the early settlers had arrived a hundred years later.
2. Devise a simple lesson plan to use to teach a new resident of your state about its recreational and scenic sites.
3. Write a letter to a retiree interested in becoming a resident of your state explaining the tax structure and other cost-of-living factors for senior citizens.

SYNTHESIS

1. Imagine how life in your state would be different today if the early settlers had arrived a hundred years later.
2. Devise a simple lesson plan to teach a new resident of your state about its recreational and scenic sites.
3. Write a letter to a retiree interested in becoming a resident of your state explaining the tax structure and other cost-of-living factors for senior citizens.

Bonus Activity:

Write a journal entry based on one of the following "springboards":

1 As I learn more about the state in which I live, I think . . .

2 One thing about my state that I find especially exciting is . . .

3 I find the early history of my state to be . . .

4 Career opportunities in my state are . . .

Conflict Resolution Activity
Bloom's Taxonomy of Critical Thinking

DEFINING AND DIFFUSING CONFLICT

KNOWLEDGE
Define the idea of "conflict" in your own words. Then write the dictionary definitions for the words that best reflect conflict as we think of it as occurring in the schools.

COMPREHENSION
Give three examples of positive conflicts that can occur between students and teachers, students and parents, and/or teachers and parents. Give three examples of negative conflicts that can occur between students and teachers, students and parents, and/or teachers and parents.

APPLICATION
Think of what CONFLICT means to you as a student. Write in the circles of the diagram below what words come into your mind when you think of conflict.

ANALYSIS
Determine what elements all conflicts at all levels and in all settings have in common and what types of things cause these conflicts.

SYNTHESIS
Draw an original picture to show what makes conflicts destructive and another picture to show what makes conflicts constructive. Relate to school-related incidents when possible.

Integrating School Success & Career Readiness
©2000 by Incentive Publications, Inc. Nashville, TN.

Conflict Resolution Activity
Bloom's Taxonomy of Critical Thinking

EVALUATION

Rate your ability to resolve conflicts constructively on the criteria given in the table below. Then rate the ability of your peers, your colleagues, or your family members.

1 . . . . . 2 . . . . . 3 . . . . . 4 . . . . . 5 . . . . . 6 . . . . . 7 . . . . . 8 . . . . . 9 10

Low   High

Rating of Myself	Criteria	Rating of Peers
	Engages In Conflicts Often	
	Knowledge of Negotiation Procedure and Levels of Negotiation Skills	
	Able to Negotiate Agreements that Achieve Both Own and Others' Goals	
	Able to Negotiate So That Relationship Is Improved	
	Able to Improve Negotiation Skills Most Times A Conflict Is Resolved	

Bloom's Taxonomy Activity
Investigation Cards

INVESTIGATION CARDS

Description:

Investigation Cards provide a tool for differentiating instruction in a classroom of diverse abilities, interests, and cultures. The cards are designed around Bloom's Taxonomy of Cognitive Development, with tasks written for each of the six levels. This makes Investigation Cards helpful in "smuggling" thinking skills into the curriculum.

Investigation Cards Can Be Used In Several Ways:

1. Teachers can assign cards to students, or students can select their own cards.

2. Teachers can require students to complete at least one card at each level of the taxonomy.

3. Teachers can also assign Investigation Cards to cooperative learning groups, with each group having the same set of cards, or each group working on a different set.

4. Finally, Investigation Cards make excellent homework assignments, enrichment assignments, or assignments for students with special needs.

You will need a supply of blank 4" x 6" file cards to prepare the Investigation Cards. Create graphic cards for the activity. Copy and cut apart the cards and paste each one on the back of the 4" x 6" file card. Then make a copy of each page of task card instructions, cut apart the cards and paste each task card on the back of the appropriate graphic card. If time permits, color the graphics and laminate the set of Investigation Cards for extended use. If time is limited, you may make copies of the task cards alone, cut them apart, and give each student or group of students the paper task cards for immediate use.

Bloom's Taxonomy Activity
Investigation Cards

GUIDELINES FOR DEVELOPING AND USING INVESTIGATION CARDS TO FIT INDIVIDUAL CLASSROOM NEEDS

1. Select an object or topic of interest to you in your subject area that lends itself to the Investigation Card concept.

2. Collect information associated with your object or topic and use this information to identify major terms, background data, or major concepts related to your Investigation Card theme.

3. Write different questions, tasks, challenges, or activities for each level of Bloom's Taxonomy using the object or topic as the springboard for ideas. Use the appropriate action verbs from the list below to aid you in developing original Investigation Cards for use with your students. With a little practice and a good understanding of the various levels of Bloom's Taxonomy, student groups will be able to develop activities unique to their own interests and needs.

KNOWLEDGE
acquire, know, quote, choose, locate, recite, define, memorize, select, find, name, trace, group, outline, underline, indicate, point, write

ANALYSIS
analyze, formulate, point out, break down, group, relate, criticize, inspect, separate, deduce, make inferences, take apart, examine, outline, uncover

APPLICATION
apply, interview, restructure, compute, keep records, solve, derive, model, transfer, examine, operate, utilize, find, plan, graph

EVALUATION
argue, grade, standardize, consider, judge, test, defend, measure, validate, evaluate, relate

SYNTHESIS
arrange, generate, rearrange, build, invent, revise, compile, modify, suppose, derive, originate, tell, explain, predict, write

COMPREHENSION
associate, group, put in order, convert, infer, recognize, differentiate, measure, suggest, extend, outline, translate

Integrating School Success & Career Readiness
©2000 by Incentive Publications, Inc. Nashville, TN.

KNOWLEDGE

You Are a Word Specialist!

Write down twenty words that you associate with the concept of "work." List them in alphabetical order. Underline each word that conveys a positive image and circle each word that conveys a not-so-positive image.

KNOWLEDGE

You Are a Vocabulary Expert!

Think of your favorite place to shop and do business. Pretend that you could get a part-time job there for the summer. Write down ten words that describe this special retail business.

COMPREHENSION

You Are an Advisor!

Pretend you have evidence that one of your best friends has been shoplifting for kicks. Write him/her a letter explaining the dangers of shoplifting and the costs of shoplifting for the consumer.

COMPREHENSION

You Are a Teacher!

In your own words, explain the concept of "entrepreneur" and give several examples to illustrate your explanation.

APPLICATION

You Are a Writer!

On a separate piece of paper, tell others (in no more than five sentences) what the benefits and dangers are of buying on credit.

APPLICATION

You Are an Observer!

Locate a yellow page display ad for each of the following resources that appeals to you and write down the name and phone number for each one: restaurant, plumber, appliance repair, bookstore, boutique, construction company, veterinarian, furniture store, hardware, hotel, jeweler, mover, landscaper, dentist, and real estate office.

Integrating School Success & Career Readiness
©2000 by Incentive Publications, Inc. Nashville, TN.

ANALYSIS
❖
You Are a Better Business Reporter!

You have just been asked to analyze a series of advertisements from your favorite magazine to determine the qualities of a good ad. Locate at least five different ads, cut them out, paste them on a large sheet of paper and determine what makes them good examples of reputable advertising for the products and/or services they represent.

ANALYSIS
❖
You Are a Problem Solver!

Representatives from the local business community have asked you to prepare an outline of what would make an effective workplace experience for students in your age group. Generate a list of different businesses in your community that would be good resources for this purpose and write down what kids would most want to see and do at these work sites.

SYNTHESIS
❖
You Are an Idea Person!

Pretend you have been asked to name several new businesses that are starting up in your community. The owners are looking for names that are creative, clever, colorful, and connected directly to the products or services they provide. Think up possible names for: A beauty shop • A pet hospital • A bicycle repair business • A video arcade • An outlet shopping mall • A movie theatre • A dry cleaner • A drive-in restaurant • A photographer • An ice cream parlor • A catering service

SYNTHESIS
❖
You Are a Designer!

Create a series of business cards and related shopping bag designs for each of the enterprises from the "You Are an Idea Person" Synthesis Level task. Again, be original and colorful in your ideas.

EVALUATION
❖
You Are a Problem Solver!

Many students and their teachers think of the word "profit" as a negative concept rather than an essential ingredient of the free enterprise system. Justify "strong profits" as incentives to both producers and consumers alike.

EVALUATION
❖
You Are an Improver!

Many older adults feel that there is a generation gap when it comes to the "work ethics" of young people today. These business leaders think that kids today are less skilled, less motivated, less prepared, and less capable of leading the country forward when it comes to the world of work. Prepare a list of statistics, arguments, facts, or testimonials that would either validate this claim or refute it.

KNOWLEDGE

1. Choose an article about business from a current newspaper or magazine. Read the article and use it for the activities that follow.

2. Write down the Who, What, When, Where, Why, and How of the article.

COMPREHENSION

1. Describe a possible follow-up or related article to this one.

2. Summarize who will be most affected by this event or issue and give reasons for your answer.

APPLICATION

1. Determine who you would want to interview about this article and make a list of questions you would want to ask him/her.

2. Write a letter to the editor about the topic of this article and tell the editorial staff how you feel about it.

ANALYSIS

1. Most actions and events depicted in news articles are part of a cause and effect relationship or situation. Decide if this issue is more of the "cause" or the "effect" and why you feel as you do.

2. Draw some conclusions as to the role of technology in this event or issue.

SYNTHESIS

1. Compose a short skit or script to act out the scenario described in the article. Embellish the information in the article with your interpretations and reactions.

2. Assume the role of an artist and draw a picture that incorporates the main idea or issue discussed in the article.

EVALUATION

1. Rank the subject matter for this article on a 1 to 10 scale with 1 being of little importance, 5 being of some importance, and 10 being of great importance to the general public. Justify your first and last choices.

2. Decide whether or not you would have wanted to be involved with the people and events in this article and give at least three to five reasons for your decision.

Integrating School Success & Career Readiness
©2000 by Incentive Publications, Inc. Nashville, TN.

USING WILLIAMS' TAXONOMY TO INTEGRATE SCHOOL SUCCESS AND CAREER READINESS

Williams' Taxonomy is another important model to use when teaching thinking skills. While Bloom's Taxonomy is used for teaching critical thinking skills, Williams' Taxonomy is used for teaching creative thinking skills.

Although there is a relationship between these two models (and even some overlap), it should be noted that critical thinking tends to be more reactive and vertical in nature while creative thinking tends to be more proactive and lateral in nature. Another way of saying this is that critical thinking tends to involve tasks that are logical, rational, sequential, analytical, and convergent. Creative thinking, on the other hand, tends to involve tasks that are spatial, flexible, spontaneous, analogical, and divergent. Critical thinking is "left brain" thinking while creative thinking is "right brain" thinking.

Williams' Taxonomy has eight levels, also arranged in a hierarchy, with certain types of student behavior associated with each level. The first four levels of the Williams' model are cognitive in nature while the last four levels are affective in nature.

It is strongly suggested that a teacher keep a copy of Williams' Taxonomy in the lesson plan book so that the levels and behaviors can be an integral part of most lesson plans and student assignments. On page 73 you will find a brief overview of the levels in Williams' Taxonomy. Each level is accompanied by a list of selected cue words to be used to trigger student responses to a given creative stimulus or challenge.

The following pages present student exercises organized to further critical and creative thinking as well as the reinforcement of basic study skills while stimulating interest in, and motivation for, increased school success and career readiness.

WILLIAMS' TAXONOMY OF CREATIVE THOUGHT

FLUENCY

Enables the learner to generate a great many ideas, related answers, or choices in a given situation.

Sample Cue Words: Generating oodles, lots, many ideas.

FLEXIBILITY

Lets the learner change everyday objects to generate a variety of categories by taking detours and varying sizes, shapes, quantities, time limits, requirements, objectives, or dimensions in a given situation.

Sample Cue Words: Generating varied, different, alternative ideas.

ORIGINALITY

Causes the learner to seek new ideas by suggesting unusual twists to change content or by coming up with clever responses to a given situation.

Sample Cue Words: Generating enriched, embellished, expanded ideas.

ELABORATION

Helps the learner stretch by expanding, enlarging, enriching, or embellishing possibilities that build on previous thoughts or ideas.

Sample Cue Words: Generating enriched, embellished, expanded ideas.

RISK TAKING

Enables the learner to deal with the unknown by taking chances, experimenting with new ideas, or trying new challenges.

Sample Cue Words: Experimenting with and exploring ideas.

COMPLEXITY

Permits the learner to create structure in an unstructured setting or to build a logical order in a given situation.

Sample Cue Words: Improving and explaining ideas.

CURIOSITY

Encourages the learner to follow a hunch, question alternatives, ponder outcomes, and wonder about options in a given situation.

Sample Cue Words: Pondering and questioning ideas.

IMAGINATION

Allows the learner to visualize possibilities, build images in his or her mind, picture new objects, or reach beyond the limits of the practical.

Sample Cue Words: Visualizing and fantasizing ideas.

Integrating School Success & Career Readiness
©2000 by Incentive Publications, Inc. Nashville, TN.

Williams' Taxonomy Activity
Analyzing a Performance Appraisal System

HOW'S YOUR PERFORMANCE?

Description:

Self-esteem is a critical element in determining one's success or lack of success in the workplace. Lynn Silton of the California State Task Force on Self-Esteem has defined self-esteem as "appreciating your strengths and skills; feeling a sense of power and responsibility for your own actions; a sense of mutual affection between yourself and others and a sense of commitment to society." In the business world, employees are many times evaluated on their work through a process known as the "Performance Appraisal System." Investigate this concept as it relates to your readiness for school success by completing the tasks below.

FLUENCY TASK:
Think of some positive, personal characteristics that make you WHO YOU ARE TODAY. Everyone has positive qualities but often we do not take the time to identify them.

FLEXIBILITY TASK:
Review your list from above and make certain you have at least one characteristic that would fit into several of these desirable areas: Attitude, Control, Creativity, Decision Making, Independence, Initiative, Leadership, Listening Skills, Planning Skills, Political Skills, Presentation Skills, Quality of Work, Risk Taking, Teamwork, Verbal Skills, Volume of Work, and Written Skills.

ORIGINALITY and ELABORATION TASKS:
Select one of the positive, personal characteristics listed above that you feel is very special and unique only to you when compared to other members of your class. Write a detailed paragraph explaining why you feel as you do.

Williams' Taxonomy Activity
Analyzing a Performance Appraisal System

RISK-TAKING TASK:
Rate yourself as Exceptional, Super, Good, Marginal, or An Area Needing Further Development for each of these self-management, interpersonal, and technical skills and abilities as they relate to your overall performance in school.

- **Attitude:** One's manner of acting, feeling, and thinking positively
- **Control:** An ability to direct peers
- **Creativity:** An ability to be original, to produce, create, and bring about new ideas
- **Decision Making:** Ability to define a problem, collect data, and reach a conclusion
- **Independence:** Freedom from influence, control, or determination of others
- **Initiative:** Ability to originate new ideas or methods without direction from others
- **Leadership:** Ability to direct and guide others
- **Listening Skills:** Ability to pick out important information and to give back to others
- **Planning Skills:** Ability to design objectives to achieve goals
- **Political Skills:** Ability to function effectively within a group, club, or organization
- **Presentation Skills:** Ability to speak in front of a group
- **Quality of Work:** Desire to achieve excellence in work assigned
- **Risk Taking:** Ability to risk change and take chances
- **Team Building:** Ability to work in cooperative learning groups and settings
- **Verbal Skills:** Ability to express oneself verbally
- **Volume of Work:** Ability to be a top-producing student
- **Written Skills:** Ability to communicate an idea, paper, or report in a clear and concise form

COMPLEXITY TASK:
Determine how effective (or not) the grading and report card system in your school is for appraising the performance of the majority of its students.

CURIOSITY TASK:
Generate a list of questions that you would want to ask the "smartest kid in your school" about his/her performance as a student.

IMAGINATION TASK:
Pretend you received the highest performance appraisal for your coursework this year in school. Draw a picture showing the elements of a big celebration that recognizes your success.

Williams' Taxonomy Activity
Climate Improvement

CREATING A CLIMATE FOR LEARNING

FLUENCY

List as many ways you can think of that students and teachers in your school could change the physical environment to improve the climate for learning.

FLEXIBILITY

Classify the proposed changes in your Fluency list and explain your classification system.

ORIGINALITY

Think of something that you could do to create a better climate for learning for your class.

ELABORATION

Decide which factor listed below contributes most to a positive climate for learning in your school and tell why you made the decision that you did:

1. Teacher attitudes and behavior toward students
2. Student interaction
3. The curriculum
4. Community and parent support
5. The school plant, books, and supplies
6. Expectations and achievement
7. Other

RISK TAKING

If you could change only one thing to make your school climate more student-centered and attractive to you, what would you change and what would be the consequences of the change?

COMPLEXITY

On a scale of one to ten (ten being the best), rate your school's present climate for learning. Justify your rating.

CURIOSITY

Make up three good questions to ask your classmates to find out about pet peeves related to the school's present climate for learning.

IMAGINATION

Visualize the present climate for learning. Take into account administrators and teachers, school plant, classroom arrangement, scheduling, curriculum, extracurricular activities, rules, expectations, and assessment. Write a creative essay describing it.

Williams' Taxonomy Activity
Climate Improvement

Reflection:

1 Relate your summary of a good school climate for learning to a good climate for the workplace. Compare and contrast the requirements of the two and draw conclusions as to how a good school climate prepares the future worker for contributing to shaping a positive work climate.

_____
_____
_____
_____
_____
_____
_____
_____
_____

2 Try to visualize what the work climate would be like for each of the two possible career choices that interest you most at the present time. How will the climate, as you visualize it, influence your final decision as to which career to pursue?

_____
_____
_____
_____
_____
_____
_____

Williams's Taxonomy Activity
Reviewing Technology in School

LOOKING AT TECHNOLOGY

FLUENCY

List as many forms of technology as you can that contribute to school success for today's students of your age.

FLEXIBILITY

Create a classification system for the means of technology on your list. Try to classify your means according to the system.

ORIGINALITY

Think of and describe a use of technology not available to students in your school that would increase student success if it could be made available.

ELABORATION

Expand on this statement, "As the age of one computer per school has given way to one computer per classroom, the next stage of one computer per student is just around the corner. Think what a difference this will make in the world of work in the next ten years."

Integrating School Success & Career Readiness
©2000 by Incentive Publications, Inc. Nashville, TN.

Williams's Taxonomy Activity
Reviewing Technology in School

RISK-TAKING

Explain how you feel about the influence of technology on the quality of your education.

COMPLEXITY

Rank the order of the following as sources of information related to global awareness and world culture: the Internet, television, and daily newspapers. Explain your rankings.

CURIOSITY

Develop a list of questions you would like to ask a renowned computer scientist about his or her prediction related to future developments in technology.

IMAGINATION

Imagine what your school would be like if for the rest of the school year students were prohibited from using any form of technology perfected during the past thirty-five years.

Reflection

How will advances in technology influence the work world that today's students will join as entry-level employees? What actions can you take now to help you be better prepared for the workplace of the future?

Williams' Taxonomy Activity
Revising Technology in Work

TECHNOLOGY IN THE WORKPLACE

FLUENCY TASK

List technology tools that are available for use in the world of work. List as many as you can.

FLEXIBILITY TASK

List careers that are extremely technology-dependent in order to be successful. List as many as you can.

ORIGINALITY TASK

Invent a job for the future that doesn't exist today, but that you feel will evolve because of technology.

ELABORATION TASK

Defend or negate this statement: "The wonders of technology must be balanced against the spiritual and emotional needs of human nature."

Williams' Taxonomy Activity
Revising Technology in Work

RISK-TAKING TASK

Share a personal experience that either tells "how technology has actually enriched your life" or one that tells "how technology has actually complicated your life."

COMPLEXITY TASK

Explain how each of the following technology tools is or could be used in the world of work: Word Processing; Digital Cameras; Scanners, Multimedia Software; E-Mail, Internet; Spreadsheets; Databases; and CAD Programs.

CURIOSITY TASK

Plan a virtual reality field trip to an Internet website of your choice. Develop a lesson plan that could be shared with peers who want to visit your site location.

IMAGINATION TASK

Imagine yourself working for a business that allows you to work full time in your home. List the advantages and disadvantages of such an arrangement.

Bonus Activity

Compile an annotated list of website addresses that provide information about careers that demand an extensive knowledge base of facts and concepts related to technology.

Williams' Taxonomy Activity
Examining Job Options

THINKING ABOUT JOBS

FLUENCY TASK

Think of as many jobs as you can that you would never want or that you think of as unimportant.

FLEXIBILITY TASK

Think of as many jobs as you can that you feel are especially stressful or difficult. Cross-reference this list with those jobs listed as part of the fluency task. Determine how they are alike and/or different.

ORIGINALITY TASK

Think of the most unusual, unique job that you feel is one of the most important jobs or professions in the United States today (not including the President, of course).

Williams' Taxonomy Activity
Examining Job Options

ELABORATION TASK

Some jobs have perks or special opportunities or privileges that go along with employment. Discuss some perks that might accompany employment as a lifeguard, a major league coach, a clerk in a boutique, a waiter in a restaurant, a model, a nanny, or a candy manufacturer.

RISK-TAKING TASK

Identify some personal traits or characteristics about yourself that would make you a very effective employee.

COMPLEXITY TASK

Create a definition for "job success" and then describe two adults you know who are successful according to your definition.

CURIOSITY TASK

Make a list of talents and skills that you think are most important to someone who has a job as a college professor, a minister/rabbi, a policeman, or a lawyer. Make a list of questions about these talents and skills to use in a telephone interview with one of the above job roles.

IMAGINATION TASK

Imagine yourself as a business owner. Describe your business and list three requirements you have for your employees.

Williams' Taxonomy Activity
Conflict Resolution

CONFRONTING CONFLICT

FLUENCY TASK

Write down as many sources of conflict as you can think of that might exist between students and teachers that could influence an individual student's degree of school success.

FLEXIBILITY TASK

Determine which of the conflicts from the fluency task are "conflicts of interest." Are all conflicts "conflicts of interest?" Give reasons for your answer.

ORIGINALITY TASK

Locate a newspaper article, letter to the editor, or comic strip that illustrates an original or unusual conflict involving a student and a school-related issue.

ELABORATION TASK

Observe and express how your comfort conflicts with the comfort of teachers or administrators. Consider your ideas versus your teachers' ideas. Consider your goals and expectations versus others' goals and expectations. Consider your freedom and your teachers' freedom. Consider your power and others' power.

Williams' Taxonomy Activity
Conflict Resolution

RISK-TAKING TASK

Map out where you have been today at home, school, and in the community. On the map, show conflicts you have encountered. Color-code the conflicts whose endings were unhappy and those that had happy endings.

COMPLEXITY TASK

What color is conflict? Draw it. Are different kinds of conflict different colors? Why or why not? What conflicts today are caused by color such as "skin color"?

CURIOSITY TASK

Interview someone who is in charge of keeping order to avoid conflicts. (School administrator, security guard, teacher, student monitor, etc.) Ask: How did the person get to be in charge? What does he/she keep order over? What makes people listen or obey the person? What methods does the person use to keep order? Where did the person get his/her authority? How does this person promote or control conflict?

IMAGINATION TASK

Imagine that you have been asked to determine the five most powerful people in your educational community. Make a list of these individuals and describe how they use their power and what conflicts you have with these people. Find out if the people think they have as much power as you think they do. Determine whether or not the most powerful persons or groups on your list will win a conflict and why or why not.

Williams' Taxonomy Activity
Safe Schools

SCHOOL SAFETY AND STUDENT SECURITY

FLUENCY TASK

Student success in school may be strongly influenced by the degree of safety and security felt by individual students as well as by the group as a whole. Brainstorm for five minutes to think of school policies, procedures, and physical features that exist to protect the safety of students.

_____
_____

FLEXIBILITY TASK

Classify the items in your safety list from above and explain your classification scheme.

_____
_____

ORIGINALITY TASK

Think up a new and unique safety policy, procedure, or physical feature for your school and design a flyer, poster, or display ad to promote it.

_____
_____

ELABORATION TASK

The results: cracked walls, broken glass, and frightened kids. What do you think happened?

_____
_____

Williams' Taxonomy Activity
Safe Schools

RISK-TAKING TASK

Explain what would be the most difficult thing for you to do if you had to administer first aid, CPR, or the Heimlich Maneuver to someone in a school emergency.

_____

_____

COMPLEXITY TASK

Which would be the most difficult health hazard for you to deal with in school: sexual abuse, physical abuse, or emotional abuse? Explain.

_____

_____

CURIOSITY TASK

What causes one person to abuse or hurt another?

_____

_____

IMAGINATION TASK

Visualize a school setting with no vandalism, theft, conflict, or threats. What would it look like, feel like, and sound like?

_____

_____

Reflection:

Have you thought about varying roles of adults with responsibilities for keeping your school safe? Define the role of each of these people as it relates to school safety:

Principal	Teacher
Security Guard	Secretary
Nurse	Traffic Officer
Coach and/or Physical Education Teacher	

Looking at Creative Thinking

WHAT'S YOUR OPINION?

Description:

The workplace is very strongly affected by women's issues and men's issues which often make it difficult for women and men to work together productively.

Some of the issues that bother women and interfere with their achievement levels are:

1. Feeling misunderstood and put down by men.
2. Less pay for the same work.
3. Slower or non-existent promotions compared to men.
4. Receive less feedback and information on the job than men do.
5. Unwanted sexual attention through words, advances, and touches.
6. Being left out of decision-making.
7. Fewer training opportunities.
8. Lack of quality mentors or coaches.

Some of the issues that bother men and interfere with their work success are:

1. Feeling misunderstood and put down by women.
2. More susceptible to stress related diseases such as heart attacks and ulcers.
3. Deprived of home and family time.
4. "Workaholic"—being addicted to work.
5. Tired of competing all the time.
6. Forced into narrow and specialized niches.
7. Not allowed to make mistakes or admit you don't know something.
8. Not allowed to show true feelings.

During the past several years, however, there has been a major transformation of men's and women's roles in the workplace. Gender stereotypes, according to some, are much less prevalent than they used to be. On the other hand, many adults are still confused, frustrated, ignorant, and grossly unskilled in understanding how to get along with each other in the world of work.

Complete the following tasks on the subject of gender stereotypes to learn more about this interesting phenomenon.

Creative Thinking Activity
Krathwohl's Taxonomy

USING KRATHWOHL'S TAXONOMY TO EXPLORE GENDER ISSUES

LEVEL I: Receiving-Attending Level Task: Divide a piece of paper into two columns. Label the first column, Girls/Women, and the second column Boys/Men. Then, put each of the words listed below in one of the two columns to illustrate common female and male stereotypes, which flow from the basic survival messages of males and females.

Dependent & Independent; Logical & Emotional; Cooperative & Competitive; Brave & Sensitive; Nurturing & Assertive; Do-ers & Spectators; Cheerful & Forceful; Focused & Flexible; Protectors & Fragile; Strong & Gentle; Implementers & Decision Makers; Fickle & Consistent; Ambitious & Modest; Soft-spoken & Outspoken; Achievers & Caretakers; Stoical & Excitable; Passive & Active; Warm & Self-Reliant; Nice & Aggressive; Cautious & Adventurous.

LEVEL II: Responding: Think of boys and girls in your various classes. Make a list of stereotype words in pairs (similar to the words in the previous activity) that seem to describe boys vs. girls in a typical school situation. Then, make a list of "Ways Girls Annoy Boys" and another list of "Ways Boys Annoy Girls."

LEVEL III: Valuing: Complete each of these starter statements (where appropriate to do so) in an attempt to validate your attitudes and beliefs about gender issues.
. . . Girls can . . . (think of things that girls can do that boys can't do)
. . . Boys can . . . (think of things that boys can do that girls can't do)
. . . I like being a girl because . . .
. . . If I were a boy I could . . .
. . . I like being a boy because . . .
. . . If I were a girl I could . . .

LEVEL IV: Organization: Write a position paper discussing (1) ways that sex-role stereotyping can be limiting for females and for males and (2) some things you can do to neutralize or eliminate sex-role stereotyping in your own life.

LEVEL V: Characterization: During the next several days, complete the following activities:

1. Listen to some of your favorite songs and find one that has a message about gender. Write down the message and describe how the message portrays males and females.

2. Watch some television shows and write about at least one incident that portrays your gender in a positive way and one that portrays your gender in a negative way.

Creative Thinking Activity
Examining Quality in Business Producers and Products

QUALITY COUNTS

Directions:

Experimenting with new business and consumer practices in the present is a good way to prepare oneself for future roles as employees. Learning good business, saving, and spending habits should begin in school since many students begin their work experience as a child earning money for an allowance or as a sixteen-year-old earning a wage through a part-time job. Try one or more of the following exercises to sharpen your workplace skills and talents.

1. Make a list of the important tourist attractions in your community. Determine what types of businesses benefit most from the tourist industry and what benefits these attractions also bring to the citizens who live and work there. Invent a new tourist attraction for visitors to your locale and show its potential impact on the economics of your community.

2. Recall a product that you or a member of your family purchased recently that you were very unhappy with. Write a letter of complaint to the company who produced it, letting them know your feelings. Try doing the same thing with a product that you were very happy with. Did you get a response from both companies and how did those responses compare with one another in terms of tone and offerings?

3. Explain the difference between facts and opinions. Select a specialized business or industry with which you are familiar and write down three to five facts and opinions about it. Share these with a peer and have them identify the facts versus the opinions in your statements.

4. Create an unusual discount department store design that has no employees to sell or check out a customer. Invent a self-serve checkout counter and explain how customers are handled when they have questions, complaints, or returns.

5. Research to find out what is meant by both of these important economic principles: *The Law of Supply and Demand* and *The Law of Diminishing Returns*. Create a simple, but informative booklet that demonstrates both of these concepts in action.

6. Generate a list of salary ranges for ten jobs that you would most like to have as an adult. Create a series of math word problems using this data for friends to solve. Try to include math operations that involve whole numbers, fractions, decimals, and percentages. Show off what you know how to do by asking a friend or family member to solve your problems.

Creative Thinking Activity
Grades

REFLECTING ON GRADES

Directions:

Read and react to each of the following creative thinking starters. Begin by reading one at a time, only once, and quickly writing the first thought that comes to mind to finish the sentence.

After you have completed the 16 sentences, read and reflect on each thought before composing your summary statement. Your summary paragraph may or may not be surprising, but it will surely help you to better understand your attitude toward grades and maybe even result in a few more A+'s on your report card.

1. I think the grading system used by our school . . .

   _____
   _____

2. Multiple choice test grades . . .

   _____
   _____

3. Numerical grades . . .

   _____
   _____

4. An *A* makes me feel . . .

   _____
   _____

5. A good definition for *authentic assessment* is . . .

   _____
   _____

6. When looking at grades, parents . . .

   _____
   _____

Creative Thinking Activity
Grades

7. *Rubrics* are . . .
   _____
   _____

8. To be fair to team members, team grades . . .
   _____
   _____

9. Homework grades should . . .
   _____
   _____

10. To me, a low grade . . .
    _____
    _____

11. The worst grade I remember getting . . .
    _____
    _____

12. Grades encourage students to . . .
    _____
    _____

13. The most unfair grade I have ever received . . .
    _____
    _____

14. I think portfolios for grades . . .
    _____
    _____

15. If students were allowed to give grades to teachers . . .
    _____
    _____

16. If I could develop a whole new grading system for our school . . .
    _____
    _____

Interview Activity
Analyzing Feelings

SEARCHING FOR FEELINGS

Directions:

Circulate throughout the classroom and try to locate someone who experienced each of the designated feelings below in a work-related study session during the past week. Have them briefly tell you why they felt as they did. Record a comment or two as a memory aid for discussion purposes in a sharing session. If possible, try not to use any individual for more than one response.

FIND SOMEONE WHO HAD THE FEELING OF . . .	PERSON'S NAME	COMMENT
1. Excitement		
2. Pessimism		
3. Disappointment		
4. Optimism		
5. Competence		
6. Anger		
7. Pride		
8. Camaraderie		
9. Anxiety		
10. Security		

Reflection:

What can you learn from observing and analyzing feelings related to work/study sessions as expressed by your peers? After reviewing your "feelings" chart, consider each feeling on the chart and add a column labeled "My Feelings." Check the feelings that you personally have experienced during the past two weeks. Analyze your own feelings as shown by the chart. Are there any surprises there?

Integrating School Success & Career Readiness
©2000 by Incentive Publications, Inc. Nashville, TN.

Critical Thinking Activity
Making Decisions

DECISIONS, DECISIONS

Sometimes it's difficult to make decisions about schoolwork, social activities, or personal matters related to school success. At such times a chart organized to list alternative ideas allows the decision-maker to consider all the options and to approach the final decision more objectively.

List three major decisions that you need to make in the near future:

Decision 1: _____

_____

Decision 2: _____

_____

Decision 3: _____

_____

Think carefully about and consider the consequences of each decision listed.

Put a star by the decision that will be the most difficult to make. Use the decision-making chart on the following page according to the directions below to aid you in the decision-making process.

> In the *Decision* rectangle at the top of the page, write a brief statement that describes the nature of the decision you must make. Then, in the *Alternative Ideas* column, list a number of alternative ideas that could resolve your dilemma. Next, decide on a set of criteria to be used in judging the worth of each alternative idea and list these in the slanted boxes labeled *Criteria*. Rate each individual criterion according to the scoring scale as shown. Finally, compile the total score for each alternative idea. The best decision is probably the idea that has the highest point value.

Reflection:

Is it difficult to make decisions about your future? Are there too many or too few career options of interest to you, or is there just one choice that you are interested in? Maybe the decision making chart could help you clarify your present feelings about career options. What other things could you do to help with important decisions that you are trying to make?

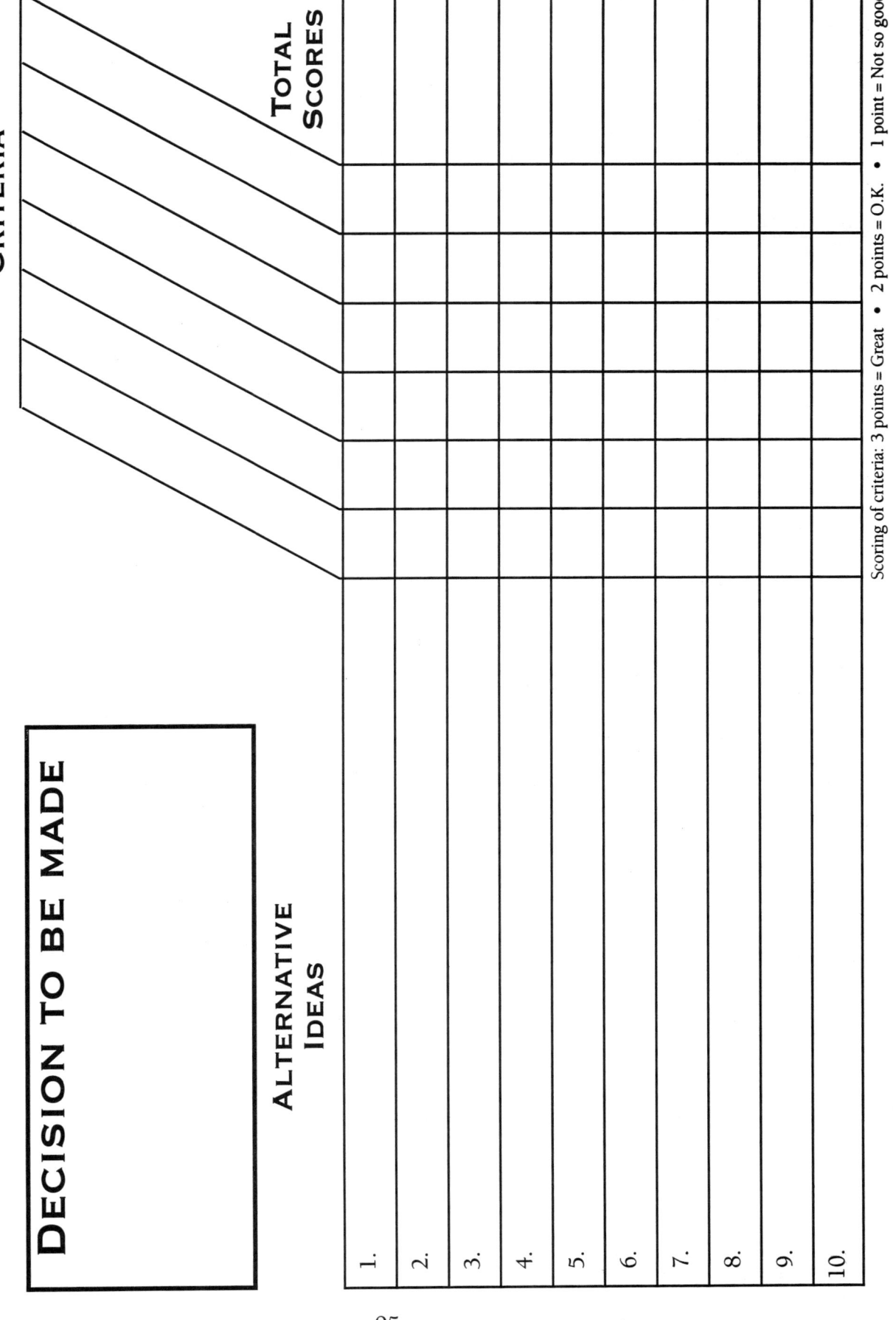

Creative Thinking Activity
Setting Goals

GOALS TO GO

Date _____

THREE MAJOR GOALS FOR TODAY	WHAT I NEED TO DO TO CARRY OUT EACH GOAL
1. _____ _____ _____	_____ _____ _____
2. _____ _____ _____	_____ _____ _____
3. _____ _____ _____	_____ _____ _____

Place a star beside the goal that is most important to you. Then, write one sentence to summarize the consequences of the accomplishment of the goal and one sentence to summarize the consequences of the goal not being carried out.

_____

_____

_____

Creative Thinking Activity
Setting Goals

List circumstances that might aid you in carrying out your most important goal.

_____

_____

_____

List things that might hinder you from carrying out one, two, or all three goals.

_____

_____

_____

Name the goal that is most apt not to be accomplished.

_____

Review and reflect on the three goals and outline a plan for the day to allow you to achieve each goal.

_____

_____

_____

_____

At the end of the day, use the following scale to determine your success in carrying out your goals.

Goal	Very Successful	Relatively Successful	Unsuccessful. Why?
1. _____	_____	_____	_____
2. _____	_____	_____	_____
3. _____	_____	_____	_____

Integrating School Success & Career Readiness
©2000 by Incentive Publications, Inc. Nashville, TN.

Brainstorming Activity
Creative Thinking

LISTS THAT INSPIRE CREATIVE THINKING

Directions:

Brainstorming is a great skill to develop as a future employee because it is the foundation and springboard for generating new ideas in a competitive world. Do some solo brainstorming to quickly list three things for each of the twenty-two topics.

1. List things that bring happiness.

2. List things that agitate.

3. List things that can be recycled.

4. List things that limit creativity.

5. List things that generate reflective thought.

6. List things that tarnish with age.

7. List things that cause discrimination.

8. List things that are flexible.

9. List things that are non-flexible.

10. List things that challenge.

Brainstorming Activity
Creative Thinking

11. List things that bring about change.
    _____

12. List things that struggle for identity.
    _____

13. List issues that won't go away.
    _____

14. List things that endanger life.
    _____

15. List things that are educational.
    _____

16. List things that threaten freedom.
    _____

17. List things that soothe.
    _____

18. List things that frustrate.
    _____

19. List things that anger.
    _____

20. List things that depress.
    _____

21. List things that frighten.
    _____

22. List things that inspire.
    _____

Reflection:

Reflectively review your completed list. Think about what it tells you about your own feelings and thoughts. Is there a message here that may help you in making decisions about planning for your future?

Integrating School Success & Career Readiness
©2000 by Incentive Publications, Inc. Nashville, TN.

Creative Thinking Activity
Visualizing Activity Careers as Identified by Futurists

21ST CENTURY CAREER CHALLENGES AND CHOICES TO CONSIDER

Directions:

According to future-oriented thinkers, some unusual and creative careers that will become reality in the twenty-first century are listed below. Note that these careers have two things in common: (1) they will generate a small number of new jobs in comparison to the overall growth of jobs in more traditional fields, and (2) they will require a high level of education and skills for entry into the fields.

Put on your creative thinking cap and consider each of the twenty careers below. Then compose a mock job description outlining what each of the following careers might entail, including educational requirements:

1. Artificial Intelligence Technician _____

2. Aquaculturist _____

3. Benefits Analyst _____

4. Bionic Technician _____

5. Computational Linguist _____

6. Cryonics Technician _____

7. Electronic Mail Technician _____

Creative Thinking Activity
Visualizing Activity Careers as Identified by Futurists

8. Horticulture Therapist _____

9. Image Consultant _____

10. Information Broker _____

11. Leisure Consultant _____

12. Relocation Advisor _____

13. Retirement Counselor _____

14. Home Robotic Repairman _____

15. Shyness Consultant _____

16. Software Club Director _____

17. Space Mechanic _____

18. Underwater Archaeologist _____

19. Space Real Estate Manager _____

20. Organ Donor Agent _____

Reflection:

Is there a job on this list that is of special interest to you? If so, do you think your learning style, abilities, and interests are compatible with the requirements for the job? If so, what could you begin to do now to learn more about the requirements and possibilities of an occupation in this field?

Creative Thinking Activity
School Success

EXPLORING CREATIVE-THINKING CHALLENGES RELATED TO SCHOOL SUCCESS

1. Write a letter of appreciation to a teacher who has helped you to achieve school success.
2. Design a word puzzle using at least ten words related to school success.
3. Outline a plan for a perfect school year.
4. Make a list of ten sources of information you could use to help you become a better student.
5. Create a profile of your interpretation of the "successful student."
6. Brainstorm some events or situations that might hinder your quest for school success.
7. Rank, order, and explain the following terms according to their influence on school success: intelligence, perseverance, creativity, ambition, and learning style.
8. Compare and contrast the effects of an authoritarian and a permissive teacher on student success.
9. Create a study guide, with pertinent prompts, for your most difficult content area.
10. React to this statement as it relates to your school success: The harder I work, the luckier I get.
11. Define the term "school success."
12. Which would you rather be, a top academic student or a top athlete?
13. Create a collage of words related to school success. Use vivid colors and stylized writing for emphasis.
14. Compose a song, poem, or other original work to express the emotions you experience when you are less successful than you want to be in a school endeavor.
15. Name and describe some teacher traits that encourage students to do their best to achieve classroom success.
16. Name and describe some teacher traits that cause students to lose interest and perform poorly in the classroom.
17. Use body language and movements to express feelings of frustration, anger, or anxiety caused by a school situation. Ask friends to identify the situation.
18. Outline the script for a TV documentary based on the importance of health habits to school success.
19. Describe the perfect school climate for student success.
20. Think carefully before naming the one person that has contributed most to your school success to date. Describe the basis of the contribution.
21. How important are self-concept and good mental health to school success? Write a brief essay to support your position.
22. Is homework an important component of your school success? Why or why not?

Creative Thinking
Weighing Career Advantages and Disadvantages

TWO SIDES OF EVERY CAREER

DIRECTIONS:

Select a job, career, or work-related issue that has two or more sides. Consider such controversial options as managed health care, welfare reform, labor unions, unemployment, tax refunds, national debt, lawyering of America, sexual harassment, exploitation of child labor laws, minimum wage rates/benefits, salary discrepancies for various occupations or fields such as doctors vs. nurses. Write down some issues on the spaces provided below. Divide the class into as many groups as there are positions on the issue to be debated. Allow time for student groups to research the issue and to develop a series of arguments to support their side or position. Reconvene the class and have members of opposing groups sit together.

Instructions for conducting this informal group debate are as follows:
1. Any student can begin the debate and offer one argument for his/her group's position.
2. Any student from another group can offer either a counter-argument or a different argument.
3. Debate continues in this give-and-take mode to move ideas quickly from group to group.
4. After all arguments have been shared, each group takes a few minutes to determine what positions were best argued and defended. A group winner is then declared.

SOME POSSIBLE ISSUES TO DEBATE

1. _____
2. _____
3. _____
4. _____
5. _____
6. _____
7. _____
8. _____
9. _____
10. _____

Creative Thinking Activity
Analyzing Negative Feelings

ELIMINATING THE NEGATIVES RELATED TO SCHOOL SUCCESS

Think of all the positive habits or attitudes related to school success that you practice on a consistent basis. Beside each statement below check the regularly, sometimes, or seldom box that best reflects your daily habits. Then select a word from "Eliminating the Negative Sack" on page 106 that best represents the cause of any behavior checked as seldom or sometimes. Write that word on the "possible cause" line beneath the behavior and make an X on the word or phrase in the sack to "eliminate the negative." For each statement that you marked regularly, write a word or phrase on the line that you think expresses the cause of the behavior.

The object of this activity is to "check up" on your negative and positive behaviors related to school success and to begin to devote attention to the "positives" that may be influencing your success in school and to develop a plan to eliminate the negative. Seriously, it can be done! Only you can "eliminate the negatives" that are hindering your personal school success.

regularly	almost never	sometimes	
_____	_____	_____	1. I listen carefully to all directions given by my teachers. possible cause: _____
_____	_____	_____	2. I complete my homework neatly, accurately, and to the best of my ability. possible cause: _____
_____	_____	_____	3. I plan my daily schedule to provide time to complete and turn in assignments on time. possible cause: _____
_____	_____	_____	4. I organize my books and school tools so that they are easy to keep up with and readily accessible when I need them. possible cause: _____
_____	_____	_____	5. I work cooperatively with classmates to find answers for questions, to share concerns, and to solve problems. possible cause: _____

Creative Thinking Activity
Analyzing Negative Feelings

regularly	almost never	sometimes	
___	___	___	6. I try to plan, phrase, and ask good questions related to assignments I don't understand or need more help with. possible cause: _____
___	___	___	7. I practice good health habits, such as daily physical exercise and a good diet. possible cause: _____
___	___	___	8. I get eight hours of sleep each night in order to be alert during the school day. possible cause: _____
___	___	___	9. I make good use of the library, media center, and content-based references to complete or complement classroom assignments. possible cause: _____
___	___	___	10. I approach the school day with enthusiasm and a zest for learning. possible cause: _____
___	___	___	11. I try to do the neatest and most thorough job possible on all assigned work. possible cause: _____
___	___	___	12. I set realistic learning goals for myself based on school schedules class assignments, and my own abilities and interests. possible cause: _____
___	___	___	13. I maintain open channels of communication with teachers and classmates. possible cause: _____
___	___	___	14. I maintain a good balance of work, extracurricular activities (such as sports, band, clubs, etc.) and social life. possible cause: _____

After you have completed all 14 items, review your responses carefully and tabulate your answers.   ___ regularly ___ almost never ___ sometimes

11–14 Regularly — Good for You!

9–12 Sometimes — Improvement needed. Consider each item carefully and think about what you can do to eliminate some negative habits and/or attitudes.

6–8 Almost Never — Danger ahead! Make a plan to "eliminate the negatives" quickly and replace them with positive habits and attitudes.

CHAPTER THREE

USING BASIC SKILLS TO INTEGRATE SCHOOL SUCCESS AND CAREER READINESS

What's the Question? (Sharpening Questioning Skills)	108
Twelve Possible Out-of-School Projects to Sharpen Use of Basic Skills	109–110
Clarifying Predictions (Using the Internet to Verify Predictions)	111
Creative Writing	112
Writing for Success (Checklist)	113
Poetry and the World of Work	114–115
Keeping Up with the World Around You	116–117
World Map	118
Examining a Company's Annual Report (Reading to Find Answers)	119
Reflecting on Resumés (Resumé Writing Practice)	120
Need for Information (Locating and Using Information)	121
Vocabulary Check-Up	122
News Words	123
Good Graphs for Good Grades	124–125
Preparing Today for Career Success Tomorrow	126–127
Timelines are Timeless (Organizing Information)	128
Who Said What?	129
Send a Letter (Letter Writing Practice)	130
Operation Observation	131
A Real-Life Application Using Estimation Skills	132–133
Science Savvy (Developing Familiarity with Science Methods and Process Skills)	134–135
Project Planning	136
Top Ten Tips for Preparing a Five-Star Report	137
Top Ten Test-Taking Tips	138

Analytical Activity
Sharpening Questioning Skills

WHAT'S THE QUESTION?

Being able to form and ask good questions to gain specific information and understand differing viewpoints is an important communication skill. In fact, questioning is a skill as useful to life in the business and professional world as in the world of school and academics.

Test your questioning skills by writing the best questions you can to gain specific information that could be of great value to you for the following topics:

1. Emergency treatment for snakebite
   _____

2. Genetic traits
   _____

3. Driver's license requirements in your state
   _____

4. Bacterial infections
   _____

5. Standardized tests
   _____

6. Requirements for membership in a school club of your choice
   _____

7. The causes of dreams and nightmares
   _____

8. Effects of exercise and/or diet on mental health
   _____

9. Consequences of overexposure to the sun
   _____

10. Penalty for breaking school safety rules
    _____

11. Measures in place to deal with violence in your school
    _____

12. Community awareness of protection of natural resources
    _____

Basic Skills Activity
Project Ideas

TWELVE POSSIBLE OUT-OF-SCHOOL PROJECTS TO SHARPEN USE OF BASIC SKILLS

1. Interview the oldest living member of your extended family to find out what their early life was like. Compare and contrast their challenges, opportunities, and options for school success with yours.

2. Read a biography of a person you admire and make a list of characteristics, actions, and events that made the person admirable. Make special notes of surprising facts you learned about the person's school life. Give special attention to the school-related decisions that may have contributed to the person's success in later life.

3. Keep a record for a week of every penny you spend and for what it was spent. At the end of the week tabulate your expenditures and review them to see how well you make use of your money.

4. Copy your favorite poem on a sheet of drawing paper and illustrate it with a border or icons. Share your poem with at least three people and ask each of them to tell how they like your poem and why they feel the way they do about it. Make a mini chart to reflect the different reactions.

5. Design an outfit you would like to own and wear to school. Estimate the cost and tell where and how you would secure each piece. Would your outfit be comparable to those worn by most of your friends or would it be unique? If unique, how would it be different?

6. Create a learning center for your class to demonstrate the advantages of a well-balanced physical fitness program for the development of a healthy mind and body. Include all necessary references and assessment criteria.

Integrating School Success & Career Readiness
©2000 by Incentive Publications, Inc. Nashville, TN.

Basic Skills Activity
Project Ideas

7. Make a list of ten things you and your classmates could do to strengthen or reinforce understanding and use of higher-order thinking skills. Introduce and substantiate your list with a definition of higher-order thinking and problem-solving skills.

8. Write a biography of one of your favorite teachers. Prepare and use an interview form to gather facts for the biography. Use your very best and most interesting writing style to make the biography into a work to be enjoyed by your classmates and as a memento to treasure for your teacher.

9. Prepare a list of questions and/or problems to be solved that will help you with a difficult content-based subject. Review the list and beside each question or problem list a reference (person, place, or thing) where you may go for help.

10. Think about where you would like to go to college, what your personal and educational goals will be, and what you will need to begin doing now to help you get accepted and become successful there. Write for information about the requirements for admission and program offerings, and write an evaluative summary of your qualifications. Even though your goals and choice of college may change dramatically before you have to make a final choice, this activity will help you focus on and prepare for your future.

11. Create a comic book for a primary grade student to encourage study skills mastery and good work habits leading to school success.

12. Create a study skills guide for your own use focusing on the content area that is most difficult for you (math, science, social studies, or language arts). Include charts, graphs, lists, references, graphic organizers and/or other aids that are particularly helpful to you.

Prediction Skills Activity
Using the Internet to Verify Predictions

CLARIFYING PREDICTIONS

Directions:

Review each of the following job-oriented statements and make predictions about each one in terms of how you would respond. Then use the Internet to research probable answers and compare them with your predicted responses. What kinds of data will you look for to help you come up with the most accurate information?

1. What do you think were the most popular occupations for women from 1900 through 1925? From 1926 through 1950? From 1951 through 1975? From 1976 to the year 2000?

2. What do you think will be the most popular occupations for women in the first 25 years of the new millennium?

3. What are today's top ten highest salaried occupations for men or women?

4. Does the concept of "homemaker" count as an occupation and, if so, what should the salary be?

5. What are the five most dangerous occupations in the world today?

6. What occupations or careers are considered to be the most satisfying in terms of service to humanity?

7. Are most people happy with their chosen professions?

8. What criteria do the majority of employees consider when defining job satisfaction?

9. Do most jobs pay the same for men and women or is there a disparity based on gender?

10. What are the most common reasons for changing jobs or careers?

Creative Thinking Activity
Springboards for Writing

CREATIVE WRITING

Directions:

Stretch your mind and tease your imagination while writing a short story, skit, or play using one of the following titles as the springboard:

1. The Job That Changed the World
2. A Career to Remember
3. A Job Too Big for Anyone
4. Occupation Alert!
5. The Work That's Never Done
6. Wage War
7. Unemployment Woes
8. Warriors of the Workplace
9. Runaway Workers
10. Career Capers
11. The Best Boss Contest
12. Work May Be Hazardous To Your Health
13. The Help-Wanted Ad That Changed My Life
14. My First Job
15. The Difference Between a Job, an Occupation, and a Career

Organizational Activity
Writing Tips

WRITING FOR SUCCESS

(Checklist To Be Used Before Completing The Final Draft of Any Piece of Writing)

Keep this checklist in your notebook and use it constantly. It will be worth its weight in gold to you!

_____ 1. My writing is neat, clear, and easy to read.

_____ 2. I have identified my reader and written so that my work will be interesting and/or informative to the reader.

_____ 3. I have presented my thoughts, ideas, and information in a logical and sequential manner.

_____ 4. I have used words that I know and understand and that will be understood by my intended reader.

_____ 5. I have eliminated unnecessary, confusing, or irrelevant words or phrases (or even sentences) from my work.

_____ 6. I have eliminated overused words or phrases, and I have avoided clichés.

_____ 7. I have used examples, illustrations, or analogies to explain or clarify main ideas or important concepts.

_____ 8. I have used some unusual or extraordinary descriptive words or phrases that add interest to my work.

_____ 9. I have included all necessary information and related details.

_____ 10. I have included a good balance of different kinds of sentences to maintain the reader's interest throughout my work.

_____ 11. I have checked my grammar and punctuation carefully.

_____ 12. I have used my dictionary to check the words that I questioned the spelling or meaning of.

_____ 13. My ending is interesting enough to leave my reader with a better understanding of my subject, some new ideas, or thoughts to ponder.

_____ 14. This piece of writing is representative of my best work and is one that I would be glad to have publicly displayed or published.

Creative Writing Activity
Poetry Exercises

POETRY AND THE WORLD OF WORK

Directions:

Write about some careers of interest to you using simple poetry forms to convey a work-related thought or message.

1. Try writing a series of alliterative sentences about several different careers. Keep in mind that alliteration is the repeated use of a consonant sound so that most words in the sentence begin with that letter or sound.

2. Try creating a shape or concrete poem about a career of choice. The descriptive sentences or images in this type of poem are written in a special shape that reflects the career in some way. For example, if writing a shape poem about a photographer, it might be written in the shape of a camera. If writing a shape poem about a heart surgeon, it might be written in the shape of a heart. If writing a shape poem about a scientist, it might be written in the shape of a beaker.

3. Try inventing a 5 "W" poem about a job option where line 1 tells "who," line 2 adds "did what (an action for "who")," line 3 tells, "where the action took place," line 4 tells "when the action happened," and line 5 explains "why the action happened."

4. Try writing a series of acrostic poems. This form of poetry is unrhymed and the physical arrangement of lines is important. The letters of the poem's title are written vertically. These letters indicate the first letter of each line of the poem. Acrostics may be made with complete sentences, words, or phrases to describe attributes or actions of the career.

5. Try inventing a parts-of-speech poem. Parts-of-speech poems are unrhymed, five-lined, and have the following pattern:
    Line 1 = one article (a, an, the) + one noun
    Line 2 = one adjective + one conjunction + one adjective
    Line 3 = one verb + one conjunction + one verb
    Line 4 = one adverb
    Line 5 = one noun (related to the noun in line 1]
        Example: A computer programmer
                 Rational yet creative
                 Sequencing and organizing
                 Logically
                 Technocrat

Creative Writing Activity
Poetry Exercises

6. Try creating a septet poem about the workplace that has seven lines and is unrhymed. This form of poetry uses syllables rather than a rhyming pattern. The pattern is as follows: line 1 = 3 syllables
    line 2 = 5 syllables
    line 3 = 7 syllables
    line 4 = 9 syllables
    line 5 = 7 syllables
    line 6 = 5 syllables
    line 7 = 3 syllables
    Example: A pilot
    Took many people
    Waiting at the airport and
    Carried them safely through the thin air
    While navigating controls
    Expertly until
    They landed.

7. Try creating a daffy definition poem about an occupation that is free verse and has no particular rhyming pattern. A definition poem is made of a selection of phrases that defines each idea or concept and that is arranged in a particular pattern.

    Example: A doctor is someone who . . .
    ——has a medical degree
    ——is often a specialist
    ——helps one fight disease
    ——makes us aware of our health
    ——writes prescriptions we can't read
    ——prescribes aspirin and rest
    ——wears a white coat
    That's a physician.

8. Try designing a greeting card specifically for a given job or occupation. Be sure it includes a couplet (two lines of verse which rhyme) or a quatrain (two couplets put together to form a poem with a rhyming pattern of A, A, B, B).

Current Events Activity
World Awareness Project

KEEPING UP WITH THE WORLD AROUND YOU

Every day that passes brings the world's people into closer contact, more connected to, dependent on, and responsible for a global society. To keep abreast of the rapidly occurring changes, students of today are called on to be knowledgeable and to be well-informed concerning current events—not just on a local or national level, but on a worldwide basis as well.

To extend your interest in the world around you and to develop a deeper sense of global awareness, select one national news show on television to watch every day for two weeks. In the spaces below, summarize the theme of the one event that appears to you to be of the most global importance.

Use a colored marker to record the date of each event on the world map on page 118. Write the date on or near the country in the news.

At the end of the two weeks, review and reflect on your recordings to gain a better understanding of what is happening in the world around you.

          Date   Theme of Key Global Event

Day 1: _____   _____

Day 2: _____   _____

Day 3: _____   _____

CURRENT EVENTS ACTIVITY
World Awareness Project

Day 4: _____   _____

Day 5: _____   _____

Day 6: _____   _____

Day 7: _____   _____

Day 8: _____   _____

Day 9: _____   _____

Day 10: _____   _____

Day 11: _____   _____

Day 12: _____   _____

Day 13: _____   _____

Day 14: _____   _____

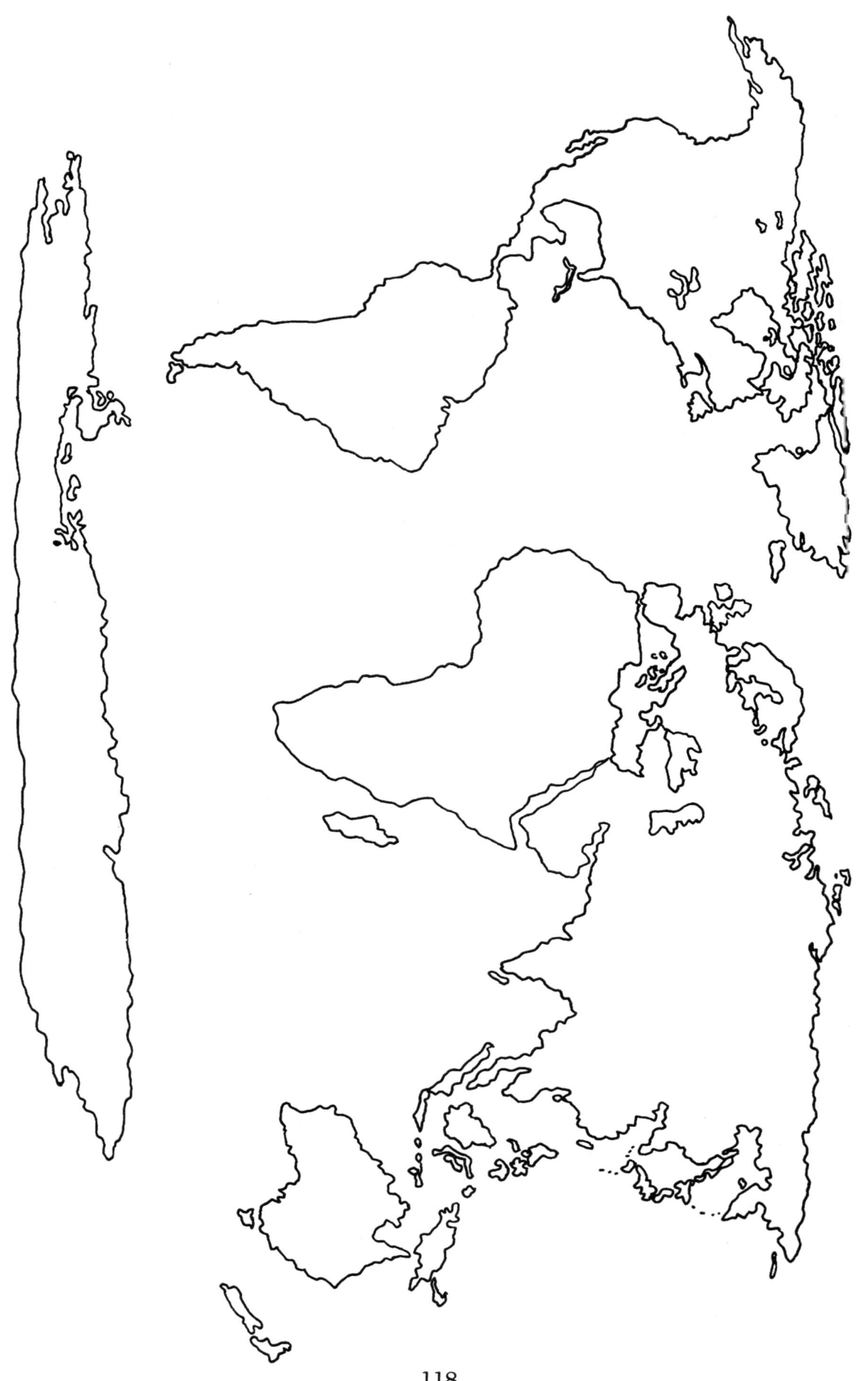

Business Activity
Reading to Find Answers

EXAMINING A COMPANY'S ANNUAL REPORT

DESCRIPTION:

Most large businesses, companies, or corporations prepare an Annual Report for their customers, clients, or stockholders as part of their public relations, communication, and/or accountability program. Obtain a copy of one or more of these Annual Reports to review and try to answer the following set of questions after reading the report in detail.

1. Who are the prospective employers and what do they do? Are they producers of services or producers of products or both? Who owns the company?

2. What has the company done or what is it best known for? What is its history? What is its growth rate? Who are its competitors?

3. Where is the company headed? What is its mission statement? What are its long-term goals? What new products or services are planned?

4. What is the company's competition? How does the company treat its clients? How does it deal with its competitors? How does it determine new trends?

5. What are the company's mission statement and strategic objectives? Do they seem realistic? Are they documented in the company's annual reports?

6. What are the company's success factors? What is most likely to influence the company's ability to achieve its targets and/or meet its goals?

7. What organizational changes, if any, does the company contemplate? How would these changes impact the company?

Reflection:

If you were unable to find answers to any of the questions, why do you think the answer was missing? Was the question valid in relation to the company's activities and goals or was the report lacking in information it should have contained? What did you learn about the company from reading its annual report? Is this a company you would like to know more about? Would you even entertain the idea of working there someday? Why or why not?

Integrating School Success & Career Readiness
©2000 by Incentive Publications, Inc. Nashville, TN.

World Preparation Activity
Resumé Writing Practice

REFLECTING ON RESUMÉS

Description:

Writing a quality resumé is key to finding a job opportunity and being selected to interview for the position. Follow these guidelines to create a mock resumé for yourself. Write the resumé as if you were just graduating from high school or college. Be creative and good to yourself. Practice makes perfect!

1. Be descriptive yet brief. Create a layout that is easy to read and doesn't look crowded or messy.
2. The first paragraph should outline the type of job you are looking for.
3. Write in the present tense when describing your current situation/position and in the past tense for previous ones.
4. The length of your resumé should be no more than 1-to-2 pages.
5. Use only bullet points for highlights and keep the total number of bullets to six or below.
6. Always start with your most recent work experiences first.
7. Use action words (strong and aggressive verbs) to describe your responsibilities.
8. Be sure to type the resumé using varied fonts and formats where appropriate to do so.
9. Use a standard 8½ x 11 envelope for your resumé, as it will make a much more impressive presentation than a standard business envelope.

NEXT . . . think of some individuals you know who would make good references for you. Consider bosses and co-workers, doctors/dentists/lawyers, former professors or teachers, friends, and relatives. Include their names, titles, addresses, telephone/cell phone numbers, fax numbers, and e-mail addresses.

Reflection:

Review your resumé to determine:

(1) Which part of your resumé would be most impressive to a prospective employer?
(2) Does your resumé present a positive picture of a desirable employee?
(3) How important do you think personal references are in the job search process?
(4) If you were applying for a job right now, what three people would you ask to be your references? Why would you choose these three people?

Research Activity
Locating and Using Information

NEED FOR INFORMATION

Since ours is the age of information, learning how to locate reliable facts and related data is more important to school success than it has ever been before. How to gain access to pertinent information quickly and easily is just as important. For practice, draw lines to link each "need for information" to the best "reference source":

Need to Know	Reference Source
The name and location of the largest city in the world	Atlas
How to pronounce and use the word ubiquitous	Almanac
The dates and causes of World War II	Card Catalog
The history of education in Vietnam	Dictionary
The exact latitude and longitude of Australia	Encyclopedia
A list of words that could be used to describe a tornado	Internet
A zip code for a friend who lives in a different city	Gazette
The exact distance between your home and the nearest beach location	Thesaurus
A Book of Irish folklore	Guinness Book of World Records

Reflection:

It has been said that in the world of work, what you know is not as important as if you know where to find it out. With the advent of modern technology, we are becoming more dependent daily on television, e-mail, and the Internet for information. Do you think these resources will replace print materials as primary sources of information?

Vocabulary Activity
Skills Checklist

VOCABULARY CHECK-UP

Have you checked your vocabulary lately? A good vocabulary, encompassing a wide variety of interesting words and phrases is a distinct asset in the quest for school or workplace success. Learning and using new words in the proper context not only makes one's conversation more interesting and appealing, it also helps in putting one's best foot forward in listening and writing activities. It's never too early or too late to assess your use of vocabulary skills and make plans for improvement in needed areas.

Think carefully before checking the rating that best fits your proficiency level for each skill on the vocabulary skills checklist.

VOCABULARY SKILLS CHECKLIST

SKILL	PROFICIENCY LEVEL			
	E	G	F	NW
• Identify synonyms				
• Identifying, using, and distinguishing between antonyms				
• Identifying, using, and distinguishing between homophones				
• Identifying and using prefixes				
• Identifying and using suffixes				
• Identifying and using root words				
• Understanding meanings of common prefixes and suffixes				
• Understanding meanings of common root words				
• Identify multiple meanings of words				
• Understanding differences in connotation				
• Determining a word's meaning from its context				
• Finding and understanding word origins				
• Developing an appreciation for words				
• Developing a sensitivity to word sounds and rhythms				
• Classifying words according to use, meaning, and other purposes				
• Identifying and using puns				
• Identifying and using idioms				
• Identifying and using the following figures of speech: simile, onomatopoeia, metaphor, personification, hyperbole, alliteration				
• Choosing specific words for a specific purpose				
• Discriminating between words with similar sounds or spellings				
• Learning new words to expand the vocabulary				
• Expanding the use of known words				

E = Excellent   G = Good   F = Fair   NW = Need Work

Review your ratings and make a plan for improving and expanding your vocabulary.

Vocabulary Building Activity
Vocabulary Expansion

NEWS WORDS

One way to make your speaking, listening, and writing more interesting is by constantly expanding your vocabulary to include new words and phrases. Use newspapers and news magazines to find one or more words new to you for each letter of the alphabet. If you are not sure of the meaning of the word, look it up in a dictionary or reference book before adding it to your list. Beside each letter list the word and the source where it was found.

FROM A TO Z WITH WORDS IN THE NEWS

	Word	Source
A	_____	_____
B	_____	_____
C	_____	_____
D	_____	_____
E	_____	_____
F	_____	_____
G	_____	_____
H	_____	_____
I	_____	_____
J	_____	_____
K	_____	_____
L	_____	_____
M	_____	_____
N	_____	_____
O	_____	_____
P	_____	_____
Q	_____	_____
R	_____	_____
S	_____	_____
T	_____	_____
U	_____	_____
V	_____	_____
W	_____	_____
X	_____	_____
Y	_____	_____
Z	_____	_____

Integrating School Success & Career Readiness
©2000 by Incentive Publications, Inc. Nashville, TN.

Graphing Activity
Student Worksheet

GOOD GRAPHS FOR GOOD GRADES

Complete the following sentences to show your ideas about the value of graphs to school success.

1. Reading and constructing graphs helps a student acquire the following skills:
   _____
   _____

2. A graph is most helpful when . . .
   _____
   _____

3. A graph and a chart are alike and not alike in the following ways:
   _____
   _____

4. A graph is preferred over a chart or table if . . .
   _____
   _____

5. Graphs in our textbooks tend to be . . .
   _____
   _____

6. Conduct a survey and construct a graph to show results in one of the following areas:

   LANGUAGE ARTS: Favorite Books and Authors of Your Peers in Reading or English Class
   SOCIAL STUDIES: Best State to Live In According to Your Social Studies Classmates
   MATH: Most Interesting Textbook Chapter or Math Topic of Your Friends in Math Class
   SCIENCE: Birthstones or Astrology Signs of Students in Science class
   (See models on the following page for help.)

   BONUS: _____

   Collect a series of graphs from magazines and newspapers. Contribute them to a classroom collection to be used as the basis of a set of discussion questions related to the use of graphs by the media to disseminate business related information to the general public. (Include a copy of the Wall Street Journal in your media resources if possible.)

Graphing Activity
Evaluating Types of Graphs

G IS FOR GRAPHS

VENN DIAGRAM

This diagram helps you compare and contrast different aspects of a given topic and record interrelationships among subtopics. Record commonalities in the intersecting segments of the circles and differences in the appropriate nonintersecting segments of the circles.

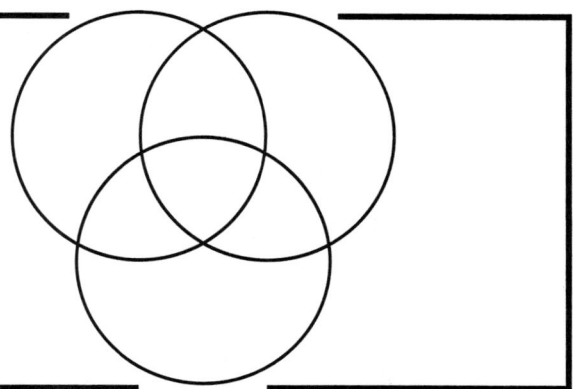

WHO, WHAT, WHEN, WHERE, WHY, AND HOW OUTLINE

Use this outline to study one specific topic. Write the topic on the first line and record the five Ws and How in the appropriate spaces in order to arrive at a summary statement.

WHO:
WHAT:
WHEN:
WHERE:
WHY:
HOW:
SUMMARY STATEMENT:

FLOW CHART

Use this chart to organize sequences of events, actions, or decisions inorder to arrive at a logical conclusion or explanation.

Integrating School Success & Career Readiness
©2000 by Incentive Publications, Inc. Nashville, TN.

Career Success Activity
Reflecting on Important Job Skills

PREPARING TODAY FOR CAREER SUCCESS TOMORROW

Directions:

For each of the important job skills listed below, write a short paragraph that both defines the skill and describes why that skill is important. Then, think of some courses you are taking right now that will help you learn and apply that skill for the future.

THE BASIC SKILLS

1. Reading Skills _____

2. Writing Skills _____

3. Math Skills _____

4. Listening Skills _____

THE THINKING SKILLS

1. Creative Thinking Skills _____

2. Problem-Solving Skills _____

Career Success Activity
Reflecting on Important Job Skills

3. Decision-Making Skills _____
   _____

4. Visualization Skills _____
   _____

THE PEOPLE SKILLS

1. Negotiation Skills _____
   _____

2. Leadership Skills _____
   _____

3. Teamwork Skills _____
   _____

4. Cultural Diversity Skills _____
   _____

THE PERSONAL SKILLS

1. Self-Management Skills _____
   _____

2. Responsibility Skills _____
   _____

3. Reliability Skills _____
   _____

4. Time-Related Skills _____
   _____

Integrating School Success & Career Readiness
©2000 by Incentive Publications, Inc. Nashville, TN.

Timeline Activity
Organizing Information

TIMELINES ARE TIMELESS

A timeline is a good technique to use to record, in an organized fashion, information or events that happened over a period of time. Learning to use timelines aids you in outlining, gathering, organizing, and reporting information and in keeping track of events in your own life. Learning to construct and use timelines in a meaningful way will be an invaluable skill for you now and as you enter the world of business and commerce.

Timelines may be made for a week, a month, a year, several years, a lifetime, or a long period of history.

Gain experience in the use of timelines by completing the following three activities in the sequence presented.

1. Begin with a week. Record just the good things that happen to you during that week.

2. Next, make a timeline to show a two-week period in your life that shows all of the important events in your life for that period.

3. Finally, construct a timeline that records the life of a person you admire (living or dead) whom you would want to use as a role model when planning your future. This person could be a sports figure, mayor or President, a parent or grandparent, actor, teacher, etc. Make sure to do the necessary research for an accurate portrayal of this person's life.

Communication Skills Activity
Guidelines for More Productive Discussion

WHO SAID WHAT?

"He said,
 She said,
 We all said,
 What did we say?"

This sometimes describes discussion groups all too well, even the best planned and most lively ones. To avoid discussions of this nature, review and rely on this list of guidelines, adding items of your own as you use it.

1. USE PARAPHRASING TO MAKE SURE PEOPLE ARE LISTENING TO ONE ANOTHER.
2. ASK PEOPLE FOR THEIR FEELINGS AND OPINIONS, NOT JUST FOR FACTUAL INFORMATION.
3. ENCOURAGE PEOPLE TO CLARIFY OR EXPAND THEIR COMMENTS.
4. GO FOR CONSENSUS WHENEVER YOU CAN.
5. BE SURE TO TAKE BREAKS.
6. GO AROUND THE TABLE AND ASK FOR EVERYONE'S COMMENTS.
7. BE SUPPORTIVE OF EACH INDIVIDUAL.
8. CONFRONT DIFFERENCES, BUT REMEMBER TO DISAGREE WITHOUT BEING DISAGREEABLE.
9. QUESTION ASSUMPTIONS, EVEN ONES THAT ARE IMPLIED, SO AS NOT TO LIMIT POSSIBILITIES.
10. CONCLUDE IN A MANNER THAT SUMMARIZES THE DISCUSSION, YET LEAVES ROOM FOR AND INVITES POSITIVE REFLECTION AND CONTINUED THINKING.

Integrating School Success & Career Readiness
©2000 by Incentive Publications, Inc. Nashville, TN.

Writing Activity
Letter Writing Practice

SEND A LETTER

The art of letter-writing is an important component of the well-educated person's approach to both social and professional relationships. Even with the advent of e-mail, telephones, and fax machines, a well-written letter continues to hold its own special place on the receiver's desk and to present the sender's thoughts in a positive and compelling manner.

To gain practice and hone your letter-writing skills, write a letter to a teacher or staff member of your school expressing appreciation for an act of kindness they have recently performed.

Circle each noun. Draw a square around each adjective. Draw a triangle around each verb. Draw a rectangle around each preposition. Underline each pronoun.

Dear _____,

Sincerely,

Awareness Activity
Developing Observation Skills

OPERATION OBSERVATION

Observation is a very important study skill. Training ourselves to be aware of people, places, and things around us contributes to social, academic, and physical success as well as habits leading to success in later life.

Observe the people, properties, interactions and events in your classroom to find answers for the following questions:

1. What is the percentage of boys and girls in your class? _____

2. How tall is the tallest boy in your class? _____

3. How many people in your class have hair the same color as yours? _____

4. What color are your teacher's eyes? _____

5. What is the exact time of your school lunch period and how many minutes long is it? _____

6. How many desks are in your classroom? _____

7. What is the name of the student in your class with the most letters in his or her full name? _____

8. Circle the word on the line below that you feel is most descriptive of the climate in your classroom.
       Challenging   Lively   Lethargic   Accepting

9. Think about your daily class period as it unfolds in this classroom. Write a sentence to tell what one thing you would most like to change.

   _____

10. Look around the classroom and weigh carefully the words you will use to describe the best memory from the time you spent in the classroom.

    _____
    _____
    _____

Estimation Skills Activity
Math Challenge

A REAL-LIFE APPLICATION USING ESTIMATION SKILLS

Directions:

One of the most important math skills that a person can master is the ability to make reliable estimations and predictions with numbers in real life situations. Rarely does one walk around with a calculator or a measurement tool during the daily routine of eating, sleeping, working, and playing. Complete each of the estimation challenges written below and then record the actual result after taking a precise measurement of the challenge task. Write your responses on the lines provided after each estimation activity.

ACTIVITY ONE: _____

How long does it take to walk from the front door of your school to the cafeteria?

My Prediction . . . _____

Actual Time . . . _____

ACTIVITY TWO: _____

How many seconds are devoted to commercials in your favorite television show?

My Prediction . . . _____

Actual Number of Seconds . . . _____

Estimation Skills Activity
Math Challenge

ACTIVITY THREE:

How many times do you blink your eyes within a one-minute period?

My Prediction . . . _____

Actual Number of Times . . . _____

ACTIVITY FOUR:

How many swallows of water will it take to drink a glass of water?

My Prediction . . . _____

Actual Number of Swallows . . . _____

ACTIVITY FIVE:

How many feet is it from your desk to the doorway of the classroom?

My Prediction . . . _____

Actual Number of Feet . . . _____

ACTIVITY SIX:

How many words are there on a page in the free-choice book you are currently reading?

My Prediction . . . _____

Actual Number of Words . . . _____

Now . . . make up three estimation challenges of your own and record them on the back of this page.

Integrating School Success & Career Readiness
©2000 by Incentive Publications, Inc. Nashville, TN.

Science Activity
Methods and Process Skills Chart

SCIENCE SAVVY

Scientific Methods and Process Skills

To uncover facts and solve mysteries, scientists use scientific methods. There are basic steps in each method; however, the steps need not be followed in any particular order. The basic components of any scientific method include the following:

- Stating the problem
- Gathering information
- Suggesting an answer for the problem (theory)
- Performing an experiment to test the theory
- Recording and analyzing the results of experiments or other observations
- Stating conclusions

When following a scientific method, use scientific process skills such as these:

CLASSIFYING: .... arranging data in a logical order

COMMUNICATING: .... exchanging information

COMPARING: .... observing how things are alike or different

CONTROLLING VARIABLES: .... identifying and managing factors that may influence an experiment

DEFINING OPERATIONALLY: .... listing the criteria by which something is defined

EXPERIMENTING: .... testing under controlled conditions

FORMULATING MODELS: .... devising a concrete representation to illustrate abstract relationships of objects

Science Activity
Methods and Process Skills Chart

HYPOTHESIZING: .... formulating an explanation to serve as the basis for further investigation

INFERRING: .... forming a conclusion from available evidence

INTERPRETING DATA: .... finding patterns or relationships in a set of data

MEASURING: .... determining magnitude in terms of the number of units

OBSERVING: .... using the senses to obtain information

PREDICTING: .... foretelling based on previous information

QUESTIONING: .... raising uncertainty

RECORDING DATA: .... gathering and systematically storing important items of information

RELATING TIME AND SPACE: .... describing how positions change with time

For school success, students need to be familiar with these methods and scientific processes and be able to apply them when appropriate. Read the list carefully and check your working knowledge of the methods and processes by making a star beside the ones you feel you could comfortably apply and a triangle beside the ones you feel you need to learn more about.

Adapted from: Student Planner and Study Guide for Science Success
(1997 by Incentive Publications, Inc., Nashville, TN.)

Planning Activity
Student Planning Guide

PROJECT PLANNING

Use the following guide for success in planning a demonstration, research or term paper, speech, essay, or portfolio entry.

Name _____ Date _____

Purpose of Project, Demonstration, or Report
   (*Write a brief statement of what you want to accomplish with this task.*):

_____
_____
_____

Description or Outline of Project, Demonstration, or Report
   (*Compose an outline or paragraph[s] describing the steps you will take to carry out the task.*):

_____
_____
_____

Special Resources I Will Need to Complete the Project, Demonstration, or Report
   (*Make a list of the things you will need to locate and use for completing the task.*):

_____
_____
_____

Timeline for Project, Demonstration, or Report
   (*Develop a timeline for beginning and ending the task.*):

_____
_____
_____

Methods for Assessing the Quality of the Project, Demonstration, or Report
   (*Create a rubric specifying the criteria to be used in evaluating the quality of the finished task.*):

_____
_____
_____

TOP TEN TIPS FOR PREPARING A FIVE-STAR REPORT

1. Choose a subject and get it approved by the teacher.

2. Make a list of subheadings and questions to find answers for.

3. Locate reference and support materials to be used (books, pictures, maps, charts, drawings, etc.)

4. Research the sub-topics and questions to be answered and take detailed notes.

5. Make a list of all materials used, including authors, publishers, and dates, and prepare the bibliography, checking carefully for accuracy.

6. Write the first draft.

7. Proofread and edit the first copy—use a dictionary and/or thesaurus and other references to check spelling, grammar, dates, accuracy of information, etc.

8. Plan the format of the report, including graphics.

9. Write the final copy as neatly and legibly as possible.

10. Carefully proofread the final copy, looking especially for words that may have been misplaced or misspelled in the re-copying. Look for incorrect punctuation.

TOP TEN TEST-TAKING TIPS

1. GET A GOOD NIGHT'S SLEEP AND EAT A HEALTHY BREAKFAST BEFORE THE TEST. THINK POSITIVELY!

2. PREPARE YOURSELF ON THE MORNING OF THE TEST BY QUICKLY REVIEWING YOUR STUDY AND CLASSROOM NOTES.

3. MAKE SURE YOU ARE PREPARED WITH THE TOOLS YOU WILL NEED FOR THE TEST (PEN, PENCILS, PAPER, RULER, ETC.).

4. FILL IN ANY REQUIRED INFORMATION (NAME, CLASS SECTION, ETC.) IMMEDIATELY.

5. SKIM THE ENTIRE TEST.

6. MAKE A CHECK MARK BESIDE ANY QUESTIONS THAT YOU DO NOT UNDERSTAND OR THAT APPEAR DIFFICULT FOR YOU. ALSO, CHECK ITEMS THAT ARE WORTH MORE POINTS THAN OTHERS (IF THERE ARE ANY).

7. GO THROUGH THE TEST ANSWERING ALL THE ITEMS YOU CAN ANSWER QUICKLY AND EASILY.

8. GO BACK TO THE BEGINNING OF THE TEST AND ANSWER ALL REMAINING ITEMS.

9. MONITOR YOUR TIME CAREFULLY, SO THAT YOU DO NOT SPEND TOO MUCH TIME ON ANY ONE ITEM AND ALLOW YOURSELF TO RUN OUT OF TIME.

10. USE ALL OF THE TIME ALLOTTED FOR THE TEST. RE-READ AND RE-CHECK EVERY ANSWER CAREFULLY FOR CARELESS MISTAKES.

CHAPTER FOUR

PROMOTING COOPERATIVE LEARNING AND GROUP INTERACTION TO INTEGRATE SCHOOL SUCCESS AND CAREER READINESS

Cooperative Learning Overview	140-144
Team Learning	145
Money, Money, Money	146-148
Round Table	149
What Are Your Values? (Recording Sheet)	150–158
Circle of Knowledge	159
Sample Prompts for Circle of Knowledge Activities	160
Jigsaw	161
Work Theories (Recording Sheet)	162–163
Think/Pair/Share	164
Think/Pair/Share Springboards For World of Work and Career Success	165
World of Work and Think/Pair/Share Recording Sheet	166
Three-Step Interview	167
The Three Economic and Societal Stages of Growth in Western Civilization	168–170
Fifteen Tools for Team Decision-Making and Problem-Solving	171–175
Ways to Improve Team Collaboration Skills for Problem Solving	176
Questions to Find Answers For When Observing a Team Meeting or Problem-Solving Session	177
Create a Co-Worker	178
Imagination When it Comes to Business	179
Learning in a Career Study Group	180
Create a Television Commercial	181
Role Models that Make a Difference	182
Investigating Cooperative Learning	183–184

PROMOTING COOPERATIVE LEARNING AND GROUP INTERACTION TO INTEGRATE SCHOOL SUCCESS AND CAREER READINESS OVERVIEW

A cooperative learning group is an excellent means of teaching basic skills or reinforcing important concepts in any content area. Cooperative learning, as described by Johnson and Johnson (1991), involves teamwork within small groups of heterogeneous students working in a structured setting, with assigned roles, and towards a common goal. The five elements that distinguish cooperative learning from traditional group work, according to the Johnsons, are:

POSITIVE INTERDEPENDENCE

. . . requires the students to assist one another in the learning process through common goals, joint rewards, shared resources, and specified role assignments.

FACE-TO-FACE INTERACTION

. . . requires the students to actively engage in discussion, problem solving, decision making, and mutual assignment completion.

INDIVIDUAL ACCOUNTABILITY

. . . requires the student to carry through on "his or her share of the work" and to contribute as an individual to the established common goals.

INTERPERSONAL SKILLS

. . . requires group members to learn and apply a range of communication and active learning skills.

GROUP PROCESSING

. . . requires the students to consistently evaluate their ability to function as a group by obtaining legitimate feedback and reinforcement.

Cooperative Learning and Group Interaction Overview

Although roles for cooperative learning groups vary, the most common roles are those of Recorder, Time Keeper, Manager, Gopher, and Encourager.

Rules for cooperative learning groups vary, but the most common are the following:

1. Students assume responsibility for their own behavior.
2. Students are accountable for contributing to the group's work.
3. Students are expected to help any group member who needs it.
4. Students ask the teacher for help only as a last resort.
5. Students may not "put down" or embarrass any group member.

The size of cooperative groups can range from pairs and trios to larger groups of four to six. It is important to keep in mind, however, that the smaller the group, the more chance there is for active participation and interaction of all group members. Members in a group consisting of two people, for example, can theoretically "have the floor" for fifty percent of the learning time, while members in groups of five can only do so for twenty percent of the learning time, if all are to contribute to the group goal in an equitable fashion. Likewise, it is important to note that groups should most often be put together in a random or arbitrary fashion so that the combination of group members varies with each task and so that group members represent a more heterogeneous type of placement. This can be done in a variety of ways ranging from "drawing names out of a hat" to having kids "count off" so those with the same numbers can be grouped together.

There are many different formats that can be used with cooperative learning groups and each of them has its advantages. On the following pages are descriptions of ways to provide six structures to be used in developing cooperative learning experiences. Each of these structures is accompanied by an illustrative student group application ready to reproduce and use. Additional lesson plans, inventories, and enrichment activities are provided to further the concept and provide hands-on experiences in collaborative learning.

Cooperative Learning Format

TEAM LEARNING

In this cooperative learning format, the teacher places students in groups of four. Each group is given a Recording Sheet and is asked to appoint a Recorder and assign other group roles. The Recording Sheet is a "group worksheet" that contains four to six questions or tasks to be completed. A team must reach consensus on a group response for each question/task only after each member has provided input. The Recorder writes down the consensus response. When the work is finished, all team members review the group responses and sign the Recording Sheet to show they have read it, edited it, and agreed with it. These papers are collected and graded.

The advantages of this structure are:

- Students build, criticize (positively), and edit one another's ideas.
- Teachers have only a few papers to grade since there is only one paper per group rather than one paper per student.
- Students collaborate on the work for a group grade rather than compete for an individual grade.

A wide variety of springboards can be used for Team Learning questions/tasks such as math manipulatives (tangrams, meter sticks, protractors), reading materials (poems, editorials, short stories), science tools (charts/graphs, rock collections, lab manuals), or social studies aids (globes, maps, compasses).

THINK/PAIR/SHARE

In this format, the teacher gives the students a piece of information through a delivery system such as lectures, videotape, or transparency talk. The teacher then poses a higher-order thinking question related to the information presented. Students are asked to reflect on the question and write down their responses after appropriate waiting time has passed. Students are then asked to turn to a partner and share responses. Teachers should prepare a plan ahead of time for ways in which students will be paired. If time allows, one pair of students may share ideas with another pair of students, making groups of four. Sufficient time for discussion and for all students to speak should be allowed.

The advantages of this structure are:

- It is easy to use in a large class.
- It gives students time to reflect on course content.
- It allows students time to rehearse and embellish information before sharing with a small group or entire class.
- It fosters long-term retention of course content.

THREE-STEP INTERVIEW

In this format, the teacher presents students with information on a given topic or concept. The teacher then pairs students and asks a question about the information such as "What do you think about . . . ?" or "How would you describe . . . ?" or "Why is this important . . . ?" Each member of the pair responds to the question while the other practices active listening skills, knowing that he or she will have to speak for his or her partner at a later time. Each pair is then grouped with another pair so that each group member becomes one of four members. Person Two answers the question using the words of Person One and Person Three answers the questions using the words of Person Four. Roles are exchanged, and this process is repeated four times.

The advantages of this structure are:

- It fosters important listening skills.
- It forces the student to articulate a position or response from another person's perspective.
- It presents multiple interpretations of the same information.

CIRCLE OF KNOWLEDGE

The teacher places students in groups of four to six. A Recorder (who does not participate in the brainstorming because he or she is busy writing down responses) is assigned to each group by the teacher. A question or prompt is given. Everyone takes a turn to brainstorm and respond to the question or prompt, beginning with the person to the left, as many times as possible within a five-minute period of time or "until the well runs dry." Group Recorders are asked to report responses from their group to the whole class without repeating an idea already shared by another group Recorder. These collective responses are written on the chalkboard or on a piece of chart paper for all to see.

The advantages of this structure are:

- It is good for review and reinforcement of learned material or for introducing a new unit of study.
- It gives every student an equal opportunity to respond and participate.
- It lets a student know in advance when it is his or her turn to contribute.
- It does not judge the quality of a student's response.
- It fosters listening skills through the rule of "no repetition of the same or similar ideas in either the brainstorming or sharing processes."

Cooperative Learning Format

ROUND TABLE

In this cooperative learning format, the teacher forms groups of four to six members. The teacher gives each group of students a comprehensive problem to solve, an open-ended question to answer, or a complex activity to complete. Each student is asked to consider the assigned tasks and to record an individual response in writing. The key factor is that a group is given only one sheet of paper and one pencil. The sheet of paper is moved to the left around the group and, one at a time, each group member records his or her response on the sheet. No one is allowed to skip a turn. The students then determine an answer to represent the group's thinking, constructing a response that synthesizes many ideas. An optional final stage: each group shares its collective response with the whole class.

The advantages of this structure are:

- It requires application of higher-order thinking skills.
- It is useful for reviewing material or practicing a skill.
- It fosters interdependence among group members.

JIGSAW

In this structure, the teacher forms home cooperative learning groups of six members and assigns each member a number from 1 to 6. Each member of a home group leaves that group to join another made up of one member of each of the other groups. The purpose of this arrangement is to have groups of students become experts on one aspect of a problem to be solved or a piece of information to be analyzed. In essence, Jigsaw is so named because it is a strategy in which each member of a given group gets only one piece of the information or problem-solving puzzle at a time. The teacher then presents each of the "expert groups" with a portion of a problem or one piece of an information paper to research, study, and acquire in-depth knowledge. Each "expert" member is responsible for mastering the content or concepts and developing a strategy for teaching it to the home team. The "expert" then returns to the home team and teaches all other members about his or her information or problem, and learns the information presented by the other group members as well.

The advantages of this structure are:

- If fosters individual accountability through use of the "expert" role.
- It promotes group interdependence through "teaching and learning" processes.
- It encourages the use of high-quality communication skills through the teacher and learner roles.

Team Learning Activity
Cooperative Learning

TEAM LEARNING

Directions:

During a Team Learning Activity, your cooperative learning group will respond collectively to questions and tasks. Assign the role of Recorder to one member of your group. The Recorder should follow these directions to complete the Recording Sheet on pages 146–148:

1. Assign one of the following jobs to each member of your group: Timekeeper, Coordinator, Checker, and Evaluator (some members may have more than one task to perform).

2. Distribute a copy of the Recording Sheet to each group member. Ask all to read the questions and tasks.

3. Discuss your ideas for each item and reach consensus on a group response for each item. The Recorder is to write down these collaborative responses to questions and tasks. The Coordinator is to facilitate the discussion. The Timekeeper is to keep track of the time allotted for the assignment. The Checker is to read through the responses orally, checking for grammar, comprehension, and consensus errors.

4. All cooperative learning group members are to sign their names at the bottom of the Recording Sheet, indicating agreement with the responses and acknowledging fair contributions to the world of work.

Integrating School Success & Career Readiness
©2000 by Incentive Publications, Inc. Nashville, TN.

Team Learning Activity
Recording Sheet

Money, Money, Money

Group Members: Date: _____

1. _____
2. _____
3. _____
4. _____
5. _____
6. _____

DIRECTIONS:

Research and write down five facts about the Federal Reserve System.

Make a list of at least ten terms associated with money. Write the definition of each term beside it.

1. _____
   _____

2. _____
   _____

3. _____
   _____

4. _____
   _____

5. _____
   _____

Team Learning Activity
Recording Sheet

6. _____
_____

7. _____
_____

8. _____
_____

9. _____
_____

10. _____
_____

Explain the difference between inflation and depression in the box below.

```
┌─────────────────────────────────────────────┐
│                                             │
│                                             │
│                                             │
│                                             │
│                                             │
│                                             │
│                                             │
└─────────────────────────────────────────────┘
```

Team Learning Activity
Recording Sheet

Create a flowchart in the box below to show the steps by which money is made at the Bureau of Printing and Engraving in Washington D.C.

Design a chart in the box below to show at least ten countries and their specific currency and monetary units.

BONUS TASK:

Draw a series of illustrations to show what each of these money phrases means:

1. "Put your money where your mouth is."
2. "Money talks."
3. "More bang for the buck."
4. "Laughing all the way to the bank."
5. "She is a tightwad."
6. "He has quite a nest egg."
7. "They have a lot of dough."
8. "Early to bed, early to rise, makes a man healthy, wealthy, and wise."
9. "I worked for peanuts in that job."
10. "What is the payoff for winning this race?"

Occupational Values / Cooperative Learning Activity
Round Table

ROUND TABLE

Directions:

During this Round Table Activity, you and your assigned group will criticize a magazine or newspaper article related to the world of work by recording individual responses to a set of five statements "round robin" style. Follow these directions in completing the Recording Sheet on pages 150–158.

1. Decide on the order for recording individual responses. Who will go first, second, third, fourth, fifth, and sixth?

2. Use the Recording Sheet to write everybody's responses to each of the five statements. After the first person writes down his or her idea, the paper is moved to the left around the group. No one is allowed to skip a turn.

3. The paper should be passed around the group five times, making certain that each member of the group responds to the first statement only on the first round and the second statement only on the second round, and so on.

4. One person in the group should be responsible for completing the information at the top of the Recording Sheet.

5. After all five statements have been responded to by all six members, the group should analyze the responses and synthesize the ideas represented for each statement into a comprehensive paragraph.

Integrating School Success & Career Readiness
©2000 by Incentive Publications, Inc. Nashville, TN.

Round Table Activity
Recording Sheet

What are Your Values?

Group Members: Date: _____

    1. _____

    2. _____

    3. _____

    4. _____

    5. _____

    6. _____

DIRECTIONS:

Different people have different occupational values or things that are important to them when selecting a job. To help determine how you feel about these values, react to each of the following statements as honestly as you can.

Student One Response

> Statement 1: I would prefer an occupation with an opportunity to work with people rather than things.

Student Two Response

> Statement 1: I would prefer an occupation with an opportunity to work with people rather than things.

Round Table Activity
Recording Sheet

Student Three Response

> Statement 1: I would prefer an occupation with an opportunity to work with people rather than things.

Student Four Response

> Statement 1: I would prefer an occupation with an opportunity to work with people rather than things.

Student Five Response

> Statement 1: I would prefer an occupation with an opportunity to work with people rather than things.

Student Six Response

> Statement 1: I would prefer an occupation with an opportunity to work with people rather than things.

Integrating School Success & Career Readiness
©2000 by Incentive Publications, Inc. Nashville, TN.

Round Table Activity
Recording Sheet

Student One Response

> Statement 2: A very important part of work for me is the money I make rather than the skills and knowledge I might acquire.

Student Two Response

> Statement 2: A very important part of work for me is the money I make rather than the skills and knowledge I might acquire.

Student Three Response

> Statement 2: A very important part of work for me is the money I make rather than the skills and knowledge I might acquire.

Round Table Activity
Recording Sheet

Student Four Response

> Statement 2: A very important part of work for me is the money I make rather than the skills and knowledge I might acquire.

Student Five Response

> Statement 2: A very important part of work for me is the money I make rather than the skills and knowledge I might acquire.

Student Six Response

> Statement 2: A very important part of work for me is the money I make rather than the skills and knowledge I might acquire.

Round Table Activity
Recording Sheet

Student One Response

> Statement 3: I want an occupation that offers me stability and security first rather than a job that is fun and exciting

Student Two Response

> Statement 3: I want an occupation that offers me stability and security first rather than a job that is fun and exciting

Student Three Response

> Statement 3: I want an occupation that offers me stability and security first rather than a job that is fun and exciting

Student Four Response

> Statement 3: I want an occupation that offers me stability and security first rather than a job that is fun and exciting

Round Table Activity
Recording Sheet

Student Five Response

> Statement 3: I want an occupation that offers me stability and security first rather than a job that is fun and exciting

Student Six Response

> Statement 3: I want an occupation that offers me stability and security first rather than a job that is fun and exciting

❖❖❖

Student One Response

> Statement 4: It is important to me to have an occupation that allows for independence and autonomy rather than one that allows me to be original and creative.

Student Two Response

> Statement 4: It is important to me to have an occupation that allows for independence and autonomy rather than one that allows me to be original and creative.

Round Table Activity
Recording Sheet

Student Three Response

> Statement 4: It is important to me to have an occupation that allows for independence and autonomy rather than one that allows me to be original and creative.

Student Four Response

> Statement 4: It is important to me to have an occupation that allows for independence and autonomy rather than one that allows me to be original and creative.

Student Five Response

> Statement 4: It is important to me to have an occupation that allows for independence and autonomy rather than one that allows me to be original and creative.

Round Table Activity
Recording Sheet

Student Six Response

> Statement 4: It is important to me to have an occupation that allows for independence and autonomy rather than one that allows me to be original and creative.

❖❖❖

Student One Response

> Statement 5: Work is little more than a way of earning money.

Student Two Response

> Statement 5: Work is little more than a way of earning money.

Integrating School Success & Career Readiness
©2000 by Incentive Publications, Inc. Nashville, TN.

Round Table Activity
Recording Sheet

Student Three Response

Statement 5: Work is little more than a way of earning money.

Student Four Response

Statement 5: Work is little more than a way of earning money.

Student Five Response

Statement 5: Work is little more than a way of earning money.

Student Six Response

Statement 5: Work is little more than a way of earning money.

Brainstorming Activity
Circle of Knowledge

CIRCLE OF KNOWLEDGE

Directions:

A Circle of Knowledge activity provides a small group situation for brainstorming responses to a given question presented by the teacher. Follow these directions to create a Recording Sheet for your group answers to the activity on page 160.

1. Agree on a Recorder for your group. Direct the Recorder to write down the names of all group members and the assigned question or prompt from page 160 on the Recording Sheet.

2. Take turns to share your responses to the question or prompt. Make sure you are ready to respond and that your ideas are recorded as given by the Recorder.

3. Assist the Recorder during the large-group sharing of all responses by helping him or her note which ideas have already been given by the other groups in the class and, therefore, should not be repeated when it is your group's turn to share.

4. Review the responses generated by both your group and the large group that have been recorded on the chalkboard, transparency, or chart paper.

5. Determine why "two, three, or four heads are better than one."

Integrating School Success & Career Readiness
©2000 by Incentive Publications, Inc. Nashville, TN.

Circle of Knowledge Activity
Brainstorming

Sample Prompts For Circle Of Knowledge Activities

1. Name some jobs that do not require a college education.
2. Identify key occupations that are overcrowded today.
3. Recall a number of careers that you would consider to be desirable. Undesirable?
4. Cite a number of work roles that you feel will be obsolete by the time you are ready for the world of work.
5. List as many skills you can think of that would be desirable in the field of teaching.
6. Determine the characteristics you would want in a good "boss."
7. Cite as many jobs you can think of that would be classified as "human services."
8. Using the letters from the word "occupation," make as many words as you can.
9. Identify the top businesses in your community.
10. Generate a list of questions you would like to ask the leader of your local Chamber of Commerce if he/she were to visit your classroom.
11. Give as many different reasons you can think of for firing an employee from his/her job.
12. Give as many different things you can think of that would motivate a worker to do a good job.
13. Name some common fears or concerns that people might have when seeking out a job.
14. State the characteristics of an effective employee.
15. Cite words that would best describe an entrepreneur.
16. Give as many jobs you can think of that are associated with the successful operation of a busy airport.
17. Cite a job for each letter of the alphabet.
18. State reasons why kids seek jobs while in school and reasons for not wanting to work while being a student in school.
19. Think of factors that would contribute to a healthy work environment.
20. Think of as many words as you can that come to mind when you hear the word "profit."

Jigsaw Activity
Work Theories

JIGSAW

Directions:

During the Jigsaw Activity you will work in a group of six in order to learn something new about work theories, and then teach this information to members of your home group. Follow these directions in order to complete the Recording Sheet.

1. Assign a number from one through six to each member of your home group.

2. With the help of your teacher, give each member of your group his or her appropriately numbered paragraph describing some important aspect of work theories as presented on the following pages. Don't let anyone see any paragraph but his or her own.

3. When the teacher gives you the signal, locate the other people in small home groups in your classroom who have a number the same as yours. Meet with them and together learn the information discussed in your paragraph so that each of you becomes an "expert" on its content. Once you have learned this information, have the group decide on a strategy for teaching it to other members of your home group.

4. Return to your home team and teach all of the other members about your paragraph. Learn the information presented by them in their assigned paragraphs as well.

Jigsaw Activity
Recording Sheet

Work Theories

Group Members: Date: _____

1. _____
2. _____
3. _____
4. _____
5. _____
6. _____

DIRECTIONS:

Cut apart the paragraphs about Work Theories. Give each section to the appropriate person in your group. Meet with the other students in the class who have a number that is the same as yours and learn the information discussed in the paragraph.

Student 1: Motivation is a hard term to define and understand. It is difficult for employers to identify it when choosing employees, and to foster it when developing employee skills and knowledge. Motivation is generally evident in the employee who works harder, more effectively, and with more enthusiasm than the average employee. Motivation is the drive. It's ambition. It's energizing. And it's a behavior that's missing in many workers. Its absence is directly related to the way managers manage.

Student 2: One theory of motivation was developed by Frederick Herzberg. In 1950, he found that certain job factors caused worker dissatisfaction and poor performance when they fell below a certain level. Yet, these same factors failed to increase job performance once they reached an optimum level. He labeled these factors "maintainers" because they maintain a level of productivity. Some examples of maintainers are salary, job security, company policies, and administration.

Jigsaw Activity
Recording Sheet

Student 3: Herzberg identified several sources of job satisfaction that he called "motivators." These include achievement, recognition, the work itself, responsibility, and advancement. Motivators make employees work harder. The more motivators there are, the harder an employee will work.

Student 4: Abraham Maslow, a psychologist, developed a famous "hierarchy of needs." He classified five different levels of needs ranging from the lowest level or most concrete needs to the highest or intangible needs. These needs are: physical comfort needs like food, clothing, or shelter; safety needs, social needs, ego and self-satisfaction needs, and self-actualization needs. As we move through the hierarchy of needs, they become harder and harder to satisfy.

Student 5: In the 1960s, Douglas McGregor came up with two opposing theories that he called Theory X and Theory Y. Theory X stresses the fact that human being are lazy and avoid work. They need to receive direction and are most motivated through fear of punishment. Theory X also proposes that the typical employee tries to avoid responsibility and wants job security above all else. Theory X organizations treat their employees as if they (1) are lazy and anxious to avoid work whenever possible; (2) need control and direction in order to perform well; (3) have relatively little ambition, and (4) avoid responsibility whenever possible.

Think / Pair / Share Activity
Sharing With a Partner

THINK / PAIR / SHARE

Directions:

The Think/Pair/Share activity on page 165 is designed to provide you and a partner with some "food for thought" on a given topic so that you can both write down your ideas and share your responses with each other. Follow these directions when completing the Recording Sheet on page 166.

1. Listen carefully to the information on the topic of the day presented by your teacher. Take notes on the important points.

2. Use the Recording Sheet to write down the assigned question or task as well as your response to that question or task.

3. Discuss your ideas with a partner and record something of interest he or she shared.

4. If time permits, you and your partner should share your combined ideas with another pair of students.

5. Determine why "two, three, or four heads are better than one."

Think / Pair / Share Activity
Sharing With a Partner

Think / Pair / Share Springboards For World Of Work And Career Success

1. Tell about the jobs you would or would not like to have as an adult.
2. Briefly describe the "ideal occupation" for you.
3. What do you see as the benefits of career education in today's schools?
4. What are some characteristics you have which might influence an employer to hire you?
5. Choose an important businessperson you know and tell something about him/her.
6. What do you think was important about child labor laws when enacted several years ago?
7. Give a cause and effect for hiring someone who is not qualified for a job.
8. Explain the "role of social security" in today's society.
9. What is meant by "sexual harassment" in the workplace?
10. How have work roles changed over the past several years?
11. Predict some jobs that do not yet exist but that you think will be a reality when you are ready for the world of work.
12. What are some major sources of disagreements between employees and employers in today's marketplace?
13. Define capitalism.
14. Tell ways that unemployment numbers affects you and your family.
15. What makes a good employee? A good employer?
16. How can you protect yourself against job discrimination?
17. Explain how you feel about allowances.
18. What factors do you think would most influence someone to quit their job and seek another?
19. Discuss ways that young people can best prepare themselves for the world of work.
20. What is the difference between a job, a career, and an occupation?
21. Give examples of how the economy impacts different employment options.
22. What motivates people most to change careers?
23. How is school like the workplace and how is it different?
24. Why do you think some people love their jobs and some people dislike their jobs?
25. Discuss how one prepares for a job interview.

Think / Pair / Share Activity
Sharing With a Partner

Name: _____

Date: _____

Question or Task to Be Completed: _____
_____
_____
_____
_____
_____
_____

My Ideas on the Topic: _____
_____
_____
_____
_____
_____
_____

Ideas Shared by My Partner(s): _____
_____
_____
_____
_____
_____
_____

Active Listening / Speaking Activity
Three-Step Interview

THREE-STEP INTERVIEW

Directions:

In the Three-Step Interview activity, your teacher will give you some information on a topic, then you will work with a partner to discuss your ideas on the topic. You and your partner must take turns as an active listener and active speaker. Follow these directions in completing the Recording Sheet on pages 169 and 170:

1. Work with an assigned partner and decide who will be the first speaker and who will be the first listener.

2. Read the information on "The Three Economic and Societal Stages of Growth in Western Civilization" given to you by your teacher. Think carefully about the information.

3. Use the Recording Sheet to prepare your written responses for the five questions. You will use these responses as a basis for discussing the subject with your partner.

4. After talking to your partner while he or she carefully listens to your ideas, exchange roles and let your partner give responses while you listen. You may want to take some notes about what he or she tells you.

5. As time permits, you and your partner are to join another pair of students and share opinions and information about societal stages of growth.

Three-Step Interview Activity
Active Listening / Speaking

THE THREE ECONOMIC AND SOCIETAL STAGES OF GROWTH IN WESTERN CIVILIZATION

Background Information:

Many economists and historians have identified three major stages of economic growth in the evolution of western civilization. They are Pre-Industrial Age, Industrial Age, and Post-Industrial Age. Four factors are considered when describing each stage: Resource Emphasis, Mode of Operation, Technology, and Design of Human Productivity.

During the Pre-Industrial Age (sometimes referred to as the Agricultural Age), people's primary resources were raw materials, and the basis for productivity was the extraction of these materials from the earth for food, shelter, and clothing. Technology of the times was very labor-intensive, and to this day our schools still operate on an outdated calendar year that implies that students must have the summers off to work on the farms. Furthermore, during the Pre-Industrial stage of societal and economic development, the overall design for survival was winning the dangerous games against nature. Could humans outwit the drought, avoid the plague, and beat the influx of insect pests to make it through another year?

By contrast, during the Industrial Age, a worker's key resource was energy, and the mode of operation focused on using that energy to fabricate or produce unlimited goods and services to improve the country's standard of living. Technology became very capital-intensive as factories and service stations appeared on vacant pieces of property from coast to coast. Designing tools and techniques to improve upon nature through fabrication, synthetics, and substitutes then became the norm.

Now, however, we have the Post-Industrial Age (often labeled the Information Age), which boasts of information as its major resource, requiring much of our ingenuity and skills to store and process information constructively. A knowledge-intensive technology will require that all people learn how to manipulate the voluminous databases so as not to be manipulated in turn by the few individuals that have those skills. A game design between persons is often surfacing to determine the "haves" from the "have-nots."

Three-Step Interview Activity
Recording Sheet

Stages Of Growth

Use the background information on the economic and societal stages of growth to answer these questions and to share responses with your partner. Be sure to record some of your partner's ideas from the sharing session as well as your own.

1. How would you explain the following terms as used in the context of the written paragraphs: extraction, labor-intensive, mode of operation, fabricate, synthetics, voluminous, "haves," and "have-nots?"

Your Thoughts: _____

_____

_____

_____

Your Partner's Thoughts: _____

_____

_____

_____

2. Which of the three stages of growth do you feel have made the most input on lives of people living in the 21st century and why?

Your Thoughts: _____

_____

_____

_____

Your Partner's Thoughts: _____

_____

_____

_____

Integrating School Success & Career Readiness
©2000 by Incentive Publications, Inc. Nashville, TN.

Three-Step Interview Activity
Recording Sheet

3. In your opinion, how has technology improved our lifestyles of today? What problems has it caused?

Your Thoughts: _____
_____
_____
_____

Your Partner's Thoughts: _____
_____
_____
_____

4. From your perspective, what are some advantages and disadvantages to workers born and raised in the Pre-Industrial Age and the Industrial Age?

Your Thoughts: _____
_____
_____
_____

Your Partner's Thoughts: _____
_____
_____
_____

5. Predict what you think the next Age will be called and give reasons for your answer.

Your Thoughts: _____
_____
_____
_____

Your Partner's Thoughts: _____
_____
_____
_____

Decision-Making Activity
Student Teams

FIFTEEN TOOLS FOR TEAM DECISION-MAKING AND PROBLEM-SOLVING

1. BRAINWRITING

Pass out a piece of paper with 21 squares on it to each team member. Have each member write down three ideas and put the paper in a center pool. Ask each member to draw a new paper from the pool and add yet three more ideas that are either completely new or extensions of ideas a team member has already put on the form. Papers are exchanged until each member's form is nearly full. Finally, ask members to read aloud in a round robin the ideas on the forms while members simultaneously cross out ideas that are repeated on their own form. Note that ten minutes of Brainwriting with ten people usually generates from 75 to 100 ideas.

2. DECISION CHART

The Decision Chart on page 95 is helpful when you have to make a decision and you don't know quite where to begin. In the DECISION rectangle at the top of the page, write a brief statement that describes the nature of the decision you must make. Then, in the ALTERNATIVE IDEAS column, list a number of alternative ideas that could resolve your dilemma. Then decide on a set of criteria to be used in judging the worth of each alternative idea and list these in the slanted boxes labeled CRITERIA. Rate each individual criterion according to the scoring scale as shown. Finally, compile the total score for each alternative idea. The best decision is probably the idea that has the highest point value.

3. PLANNING TREE

Use the Planning Tree as a tool for planning and completing a project that has a major goal and sub-goals to accomplish a variety of sequential tasks. Write your major goal in a large box. Finally, organize the sequence of tasks for the implementation of the goals in smaller boxes. It is important that each set of tasks be grouped with the appropriate sub-goal in the diagram.

Decision-Making Activity
Student Teams

4. CAUSE AND EFFECT CHAIN

Create a Cause and Effect Chain to record a series of cause-and-effect relationships learned from a topic of study. Be sure that each CAUSE produces a related EFFECT and that all of the CAUSES lead to the ultimate or final EFFECT.

5. COMPARE AND CONTRAST DIAGRAM

Use a Compare and Contrast Diagram when you want to relate a new concept you are researching or learning to knowledge you already have on a related concept. Concept 1 and Concept 2 should be recorded in two rectangles at the top of the page.

Comparison Step: Write how the two concepts are similar in a box labeled
        HOW ALIKE?

Contrast Step: Write the differences between the two concepts in the
        HOW DIFFERENT? columns.

6. FISHBONE MODEL

The Fishbone Model is good to use when investigating the causes of a research problem that involves a cause-and-effect situation. The effect is written in the rectangle at the HEAD of the fish and various categories are written in the rectangles at the ends of the major BONES of the fish. Possible causes of the effect are recorded on the SMALLER BONES under the most appropriate category names.

Decision-Making Activity
Student Teams

7. FLOWCHARTS

Flowcharts are used to organize sequences of events, actions, or decisions. A standard set of symbols is used when designing flowcharts so that all can understand them. The arrangement of the symbols will vary according to the type of sequence depicted. The symbols and how each one is used are explained. Use a blank piece of paper to create your flowchart.

8. ISSUE IDENTIFICATION AND CLASSIFICATION DIAGRAM

An Issue Identification and Classification Diagram is especially helpful when a small group of students is analyzing a large or complex issue in social studies, current events, or science classes (such as prejudice, crime, or pollution). It is a good way to organize and understand thoughts and ideas related to issues that may be difficult to grasp.

9. OPPOSING FORCES CHART

An Opposing Forces Chart is best used in small groups. Use it when you are trying to identify potential causes of and solutions for a problem or important challenge/opportunity. At the top of the chart, write the situation to be resolved or challenge/opportunity goal to be reached. In the arrows under the DRIVING FORCES heading, record as many forces as you can that you think would move you toward your goal or problem solution. (Driving forces are defined as positive actions, skills, people, tools, and procedures available to you at this time.) In the arrows under the OPPOSING FORCES heading, record as many forces as you can that you think are keeping you from reaching your goal or solving your problem. (Opposing forces can be any restraining actions, skills, people, tools, and procedures that are interfering with your attempts to resolve your situation.) Once the forces have been identified, it is up to you to prioritize the driving and opposing forces and to begin eliminating the problem areas and capitalizing on the positive areas.

Decision-Making Activity
Student Teams

---

10. ORGANIZING TREE

Use an Organizing Tree to organize information and structure your ideas on a topic in any content area. Write the major topic in the oval at the top of the tree, subheadings in other ovals, and information on diagonals extending from the subheadings.

---

11. DISCUSSION GUIDE

When evaluating new ideas, using a Discussion Guide can help in formulating your opinion of an issue. For each statement or idea to be discussed, record your initial response. Then, share your thoughts by discussing them with a partner. After you have finished, revise your opinions as needed and be prepared to discuss your responses with the entire team.

---

12. DELPHI METHOD

Each team member independently and anonymously writes down comments and suggestions about ways to deal with a problem, issue, or decision. Ideas are then compiled, reproduced, and distributed to team members for observation and reaction. Next, each member provides feedback to the entire team concerning each of the comments and proposed solutions or decisions. Finally, the members reach consensus on which solution or decision is most acceptable to the team as a whole.

Decision-Making Activity
Student Teams

13. MULTI-VOTING

Each person on the team votes for as many ideas as he or she likes. The ideas that get the most votes are circled. The remaining votes are consolidated where possible to do so. Each person then votes again, but this time for only half the number of ideas that are circled. Multivoting continues until the list is down to no more than three to five ideas.

14. NOMINAL GROUP VOTING

Use this technique as a good alternative to multi-voting or use it to further reduce and prioritize the discussion options. Assume that the multi-voting exercise resulted in six items remaining and there was not time enough to discuss for consensus. The facilitator then asks each team member to rate the remaining items from "1" to "6" on a 3 x 5 card or Post-It™ note. The "6" represents the item they most favor and "1" the least favored. These ratings are then tabulated on a flipchart by the recorder. The highest scored item represents the team's greatest support. After discussion, the team is asked if it can fully support this item.

15. THE DOT TECHNIQUE

The group brainstorms a number of items. Each member of the group receives three stick-em dots: one red, one yellow, and one green. A red dot equals three points; a yellow dot equals two points; and a green dot equals one point. Team members then "spend" their three dots by placing them on the master list of brainstormed items. If a person feels strongly about one item, all three dots can be placed on that item, but if a person prefers to spread their feelings around then he/she can spread the dots over three different items. The value of the dots is then tallied for each item and the results of the tally are discussed. The "dot procedure" can be repeated to reduce the number of items if necessary. All items receiving at least one red dot (someone's highest ranking) should remain on the list for further discussion and voting.

Collaboration Skills Activity
Problem-Solving Tips

WAYS TO IMPROVE TEAM COLLABORATION SKILLS FOR PROBLEM SOLVING

1. Conduct short and simple warm-up activities or exercises at every team meeting to get across the idea that problem solving can be fun.

2. Permit and encourage "off the wall" and "out of the box" thinking.

3. Post team collaboration skills on the wall for all to see and refer to during a problem-solving session.

4. Schedule visitations to observe the creative process skills in outside groups.

5. Invite an outside facilitator to act as a referee and catalyst to eliminate barriers to creative problem solving.

6. Make the ambience for the meeting place more creative by moving furniture, playing games, wearing costumes, giving out toys or novelties, or doing something unexpected.

7. Conduct some action research on the problem you are trying to solve by visiting the problem where it happens, interviewing people involved with the problem, performing problem tasks, or experiencing the problems as the recipient of the problem.

8. Think of some respected figure in the school that has a great reputation for creativity, ideas, and uniqueness. Ask the team to think about how that person would address the problem.

Group Evaluation Activity
Questions to Answer

QUESTIONS TO FIND ANSWERS FOR WHEN OBSERVING A TEAM MEETING OR PROBLEM-SOLVING SESSION

To obtain an objective opinion about how a team is functioning, an outside observer may be recruited (an administrator, teacher of another class, or parent might be asked to fill this role) to sit in on a team meeting or problem-solving session. The following questions can be used to record the behaviors of the group members and the group processing outcomes.

1. Did the team get started on time and how was this accomplished?
2. How well did the team set up its agenda and structure for the meeting?
3. How did the team establish their rules and/or follow their predetermined procedures?
4. How did the team share information and explore different perspectives or points of view?
5. How did the team handle conflict?
6. How did the team stay on task?
7. How were ideas accepted, rejected, and/or recorded?
8. How were decisions made?
9. How was consensus achieved?
10. How active and widespread was the participation of team members?
11. How did the team reflect on its own functioning?
12. How did the team leader or facilitator maintain order, control, and/or time on task?
13. What type of climate emerged?
14. What type of minutes or records were kept?
15. How were follow-up tasks and timelines delegated or handled?

Integrating School Success & Career Readiness
©2000 by Incentive Publications, Inc. Nashville, TN.

Creative Thinking Activity
Defining Cooperative Traits

CREATE A CO-WORKER

Just as great sports teams are built only by teams of players who have learned to plan and work together, so are great work teams made. Stars are important and affect team success greatly, yet the supporting members of the team are equally important in setting and achieving the team's end goals.

Complete the activity below to help you think through the traits important to being a good team player in a co-operative work group.

Imagine that you could create the perfect co-worker.
Describe your creation in the spaces provided.

Personal Qualities: _____
_____
_____

Talents and Abilities: _____
_____
_____

Professional Habits: _____
_____
_____

Other Important Traits: _____
_____
_____
_____

Now reflect on your own traits and abilities. How do you rate as a co-worker?
_____
_____
_____
_____

Creative Thinking Activity
Student Sheet

IMAGINATION WHEN IT COMES TO BUSINESS

Directions:

One of the things that CEO's of Fortune 500 Companies feel is most important in the employees they hire today is the set of competencies known as "creativity or creative thinking skills." To test you on your ability to "think outside the box," work in a small cooperative learning group, and complete each of the short, but sometimes difficult and imaginative challenges below. Respect all contributions from group members and reach group consensus before writing answers to the questions. Share and discuss responses with the total group.

1. What shape is an entrepreneur?

2. What does profit look like?

3. What color is credit?

4. What does a consumer sound like?

5. What is the weight of a "good buy?"

6. What is the distance of money?

7. What is the texture of discrimination?

8. What do employee relationships feel like?

Student Group Activity
Planning Guide

LEARNING IN A CAREER STUDY GROUP

Directions:

According to study group experts, a study group is "a small number of individuals joining together to increase their capacities through new learning for the benefit of personal growth." Follow these steps in forming study groups that could be organized to examine various career choices.

1. Keep the size of the group to no more than six to keep the study group process manageable.
2. Keep a regular schedule on a weekly basis.
3. Establish group rules at the first meeting of the study group so that every member understands and supports the rules and follows the acceptable standards for behavior.
4. Agree on an action plan for the study group and adjust the timeline and tasks on a need basis.
5. Complete a log after each study group meeting that provides a written summary of what happened at a study group meeting. This gives the study group a history or track record.
6. Encourage members to keep individual logs for their personal reflections.
7. Establish a pattern of study group leadership that encourages each member to serve as the study group leader on a rotating basis.
8. Make a comprehensive list of varied material and human resources.
9. Consider a variety of data sources as part of the action plan, including such options as reference books, video or audiotapes, Internet, interviews, field trips, speakers, and magazines or journals.
10. Evaluate the effectiveness of the study group.

Set aside a day for individual study groups to share their findings with the total group. This sharing session will accomplish several objectives, among which are:
(1) dissemination of knowledge; (2) evaluation of individual group activity; and
(3) opportunity or creative presentations.

Small Group Activity
Creative Thinking

CREATE A TELEVISION COMMERCIAL

Directions:

Work with a small group of peers and follow these steps to complete the task outlined below:

1. Discuss your favorite television commercials and give reasons why they are special.

2. Describe ways that producers of television commercials use gimmicks to make their messages creative and appealing. Consider such elements as humor, sex appeal, animation, well-known personalities, slogans, music, comparisons, figurative language, and surprises.

3. Create a thirty-to-sixty second television commercial that advertises and promotes a career of interest to you at the present time.

4. Perform your television commercial for an audience of peers or parents/guardians.

5. Create a print version of your television commercial and post it on the classroom bulletin boards or walls.

6. Draw a rough sketch and write the script for your television commercial idea.

Cooperative Learning Activity
Student Sheet

ROLE MODELS THAT MAKE A DIFFERENCE

Directions:

Work with a small cooperative learning group to define and determine what makes a good role model. As a group, brainstorm and agree on three national or international business leaders and three national or international companies that you admire. List the characteristics of each leader and business as well as contributions each has made to society at large. Reach consensus on a good definition of a role model for students of your age. Then write the definition in the space provided. Using your definition, list the qualities that influenced you to choose the three role models selected. Write these traits in the box. In a total class discussion, compare definitions and traits of all groups. Look for similarities and differences. Select one person as the "Super Role Model," best fitting the criteria as determined by the total group after reviewing all names on all lists.

Definition of Role Model: _____
_____
_____
_____

Positive Traits of Role Models Selected
1. _____
2. _____
3. _____
4. _____
5. _____

Integrating School Success & Career Readiness
©2000 by Incentive Publications, Inc. Nashville, TN.

Cooperation Activity
Cooperative Learning

INVESTIGATING COOPERATIVE LEARNING

ACTIVITY ONE:

As an individual, rate how you feel about cooperating with others. What are your major actions and reactions most likely to be?

| I tend to avoid group activities or meetings involving teachers (or parents). | I take part in group activities or meetings involving teachers (or parents) as often as possible. |

| I'm never the first person to start a conversation with a teacher (or parent). | I go out of my way to start conversations with other teachers (or parents). |

| I prefer to be alone when I meet with a teacher (or parent). | I avoid being alone when I meet with a teacher (or parent). |

| When I'm in a group or conversation with a teacher (or parent) I don't contribute much. | I contribute a lot to every group or conversation I'm involved in. |

| I am not an important group member. | My membership in a group is always important. |

ACTIVITY TWO:

Describe one cooperative thing you did this week in school and record something you often say that encourages cooperative thinking.

Integrating School Success & Career Readiness
©2000 by Incentive Publications, Inc. Nashville, TN.

Cooperation Activity
Cooperative Learning

ACTIVITY THREE:

Participate with a group of peers in this activity which demonstrates the power of cooperative behavior. Sit in a circle. Give each person three toothpicks. Hand a bottle to one person in each group. Direct that person to place one toothpick across the opening of the bottle and pass the bottle to the next person. Have that person repeat the procedure, using one toothpick. Continue passing the bottle around the circle, adding one toothpick at a time until all of the toothpicks have been successfully placed across the opening of the bottle. The rule is that if even one toothpick drops, the game must start over. Record how long it takes each group to successfully complete the task. Discuss how cooperative behaviors helped the group complete the task.

ACTIVITY FOUR:

With a group of five or six peers sit around a table. Select one member to be the Observer. Announce that all other team members are Players. The Observer's job is to observe how well the group works together. In preparing for this activity provide eight 8-inch-by-8-inch squares of construction paper or oak tag. Individually cut each square into three to five smaller pieces (see illustration which follows). Place all of the pieces for one team in a single envelope. Read the following game rules aloud: (1) Your task is to assemble eight squares of EQUAL size. (2) There will be NO talking, pointing, or other nonverbal communication. (3) A player may pass puzzle parts to any other team member at any time. (4) You may NOT take, ask for, or indicate in any way that you want another team member's puzzle pieces. (5) There is no time limit. The game is over when you have finished.

Distribute the puzzle pieces randomly among the players and give each player approximately the same number of pieces. Give the signal to start play. At the conclusion of the activity, discuss how cooperation played a major role in getting the job done!

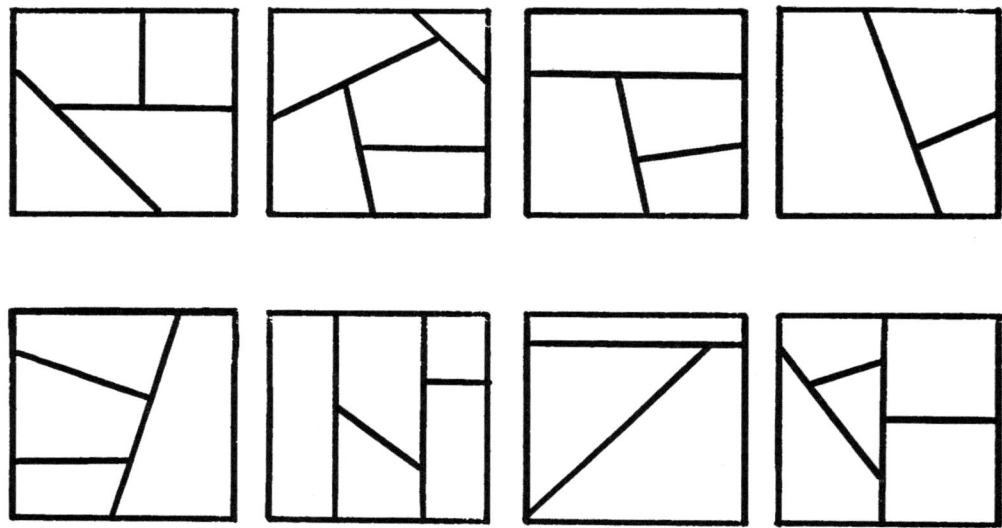

CHAPTER FIVE

FACILITATING AUTHENTIC ASSESSMENT TO INTEGRATE SCHOOL SUCCESS AND CAREER READINESS

Facilitating Authentic Assessment	186–187
Self-Analysis of My Readiness to be a Classroom Career Expert	188–189
Questions Apt to Be Asked During a Job Interview	190
Fast-Paced Changes in the Workplace (Product Assessment)	191
The Workplace Collage	192
School Success is No Accident (Suggestions for Success)	193–194
Ten Possible Product Challenges	195
Ten Product/Performance Projects	196
Six Performances to Showcase What You Have Learned About Career Education	197
Ten Career Book Projects to Create	198
Suggested Journal Topics	199
Communication Countdown	200
Interviews are Important (Interview/Performance Assessment)	201
Self-Help options for Looking at Career Clusters (Independent Project)	202
Portfolio Rubric	203
Rubric for Assessing the Quality of an Independent or Group Project, Product, or Performance	204
The ABC's of What I've Learned About the World of Work	205–206

FACILITATING AUTHENTIC ASSESSMENT

In comparison with traditional types of assessment, assessment practices today emphasize more authentic ways to demonstrate that student learning has taken place. There is less assessment of the recall of information and more of the processing of information. Collecting evidence about a student over time in realistic settings is the best way to document growth and acquisition of both skills and content.

Product, performance, and portfolio assessment offer alternative assessment methods. They are all more authentic than traditional methods because they:

- Require collaboration among student, teacher, and peers
- Encourage student ownership through self-assessment
- Set flexible time limits
- Are scored through multi-faceted systems
- Allow for student strengths and weaknesses
- Make use of individual learning styles and interests
- Minimize competition

In short, authentic assessment is designed to reflect real-world applications of knowledge whenever possible.

PRODUCT ASSESSMENT
   . . . requires the student to produce a concrete end result. This can take many forms, ranging from a videotape or experiment to an exhibit or report.

PERFORMANCE ASSESSMENT
   . . . requires the student to actively demonstrate a set of skills and processes while performing a pre-determined task.

PORTFOLIO ASSESSMENT
   . . . requires the student to maintain a collection of artifacts that reflects the student's overall efforts, progress, and achievements in one or more areas. It is important to note that both products and performances can and should become artifacts contained within the portfolio itself.

Assessment is also made more authentic through the consistent use of *rubrics* and *metacognitive reflections* throughout the assessment experience.

Rubrics are checklists that contain sets of criteria for measuring the elements of a product, performance, or portfolio. They can be designed as a qualitative measure (holistic rubric) to gauge overall performance to a prompt, or they can be designed as a quantitative measure (analytic rubric) to award points for each of several elements in a response to a prompt.

Metacognitive reflections are self-assessment observations and statements made by the individual student about each product or performance that he or she has completed. These reflections become part of the portfolio contents.

Although authentic assessment is designed to enhance and support the curriculum rather than dictate or limit the curriculum, it should be noted that more traditional types of measurements such as paper/pencil quizzes, objective end-of-chapter tests, and standardized achievement exams continue to play an important role in today's assessment practices. They may become one type of artifact included in the portfolio, one type of grade assigned to a performance, or one type of measure used to determine the value of a product. It should be further noted that traditional tests continue to be an integral part of the school assessment program, as well as an expected aspect of the world of work (especially at the entry level). Learning to deal with and master traditional tests is vital to student success. Equipping the test taker with the skills necessary to relieve anxiety and master traditional test taking situations is still an important component of the schooling process.

Self-Assessment Activity
Classroom Career Expert

SELF-ANALYSIS OF MY READINESS TO BE A CLASSROOM CAREER EXPERT

Procedural Suggestion:

The items listed below ask you to self-assess your current state of readiness for taking on the role of student advisor or expert for a career you have studied in depth. Complete each item. Be honest in your rankings and be ready to share your reasons for each choice.

1. I enjoy teaching and/or facilitating the learning of key concepts, skills, attitudes, and beliefs associated with a specific career.

   Usually   Sometimes   Rarely

2. I am comfortable and willing to share my personal feelings and experiences with my peers.

   Usually   Sometimes   Rarely

3. I show considerable interest in and enthusiasm for the career I have studied.

   Usually   Sometimes   Rarely

4. I am willing to try new things and take reasonable risks with my career-related responsibilities.

   Usually   Sometimes   Rarely

5. I am prepared and organized when talking about my career research.

   Usually   Sometimes   Rarely

Self-Assessment Activity
Classroom Career Expert

6. I look forward to each opportunity when serving as a career expert.
       Usually   Sometimes   Rarely

7. I can spark students' interest in the challenges and purposes of the career I
       Usually   Sometimes   Rarely

8. I believe that all students can benefit from my career expertise.
       Usually   Sometimes   Rarely

9. I am a positive role model as a career expert in my classroom.
       Usually   Sometimes   Rarely

10. I learn more about the topic I am sharing by carefully preparing for the sharing session, double checking facts, making notes, and rehearsing ahead of time.
        Usually   Sometimes   Rarely

Reflection:

Read over your ratings to determine how good your leadership skills and ability to take charge of a teaching situation are. Think about and discuss how these skills will impact your success in the world of work.

What can you do to begin improving your abilities for facilitating an instructional situation that will result in success for all concerned?

Interview Activity
Student Practice

QUESTIONS APT TO BE ASKED DURING A JOB INTERVIEW

Directions:

Try writing the answers you would honestly give for each of the possible interview questions that you might be asked during a job interview. Your answers may help you understand and make use of your own strengths and interests.

1. Tell me about yourself.

2. What special qualities do you bring to this job?

3. What are your primary strengths and weaknesses?

4. How well do you perform under pressure?

5. Are you a team player or do you prefer to work on your own?

6. Tell me about your extracurricular activities.

7. What type of student are/were you? What kind of grades did you receive? What subjects were of most interest to you?

8. How would your teachers describe you? Your parents or guardians? Your friends?

9. Have you ever volunteered for any organization or institution? If so, which ones?

10. Have you ever received any special honors or awards? If so, what were they for?

11. Describe your ideal boss and/or job situation.

12. What do you want most out of your job? Money? Satisfaction? Power? Opportunity?

Creative Thinking Activity
Work Habits

FAST-PACED CHANGES IN THE WORKPLACE

Directions:

Use the following facts and quotations to stimulate your thinking about the new work habits for the radically changing world of work. Reflect on these ideas and discuss them with a peer. Write a journal article or brief essay on how you think these changes will impact students of your age when they are ready to join the adult workforce. Include information on to how you could begin to be prepared to meet these challenges in a positive way.

1. In the next 50 years, less than half the workforce in the industrial world will be holding conventional full-time jobs in organizations. Those full-timers or insiders will be the new minority.
2. Every year more and more people will be self-employed.
3. There has been more information produced in the last 30 years than during the previous 5000.
4. The available information supply doubles every three to five years.
5. The cost of computing power drops roughly 30% every year and microchips are doubling in performance power every 18 months.
6. Today's average consumers wear more computing power on their wrists than existed in the entire world before 1961.
7. Constant training, re-training, job hopping, and even career hopping will become the norm.
8. It's estimated that the U.S. will generate 10,000 new jobs per day for the next decade, but few (if any) in the manufacturing sector. A similar process is transforming the European and Japanese economies. World exports of services and "intellectual property" are now equal to those of electronics and autos combined, or of the combined exports in food and fuels.
9. The annual rate of growth for World Wide Web traffic is 341,000 percent. Approximately 159 countries are reachable by electronic mail.
10. Within the next decade, education will change more than it has changed since the printed book created the modern school over 300 years ago. Education can no longer be confined to the schools. Every employing institution has to become a teacher.

Sources: Pritchett, P. (1994). The employee handbook of new work habits for a radically changing world. Dallas, TX: Pritchett & Associates, Inc. Reprint used with full permission of Pritchett & Associates. All rights are reserved.

Pritchett, P. (1996). Mindshift: The employee handbook for understanding the changing world of work. Dallas, TX: Pritchett & Associates, Inc. Reprint used with full permission of Pritchett & Associates. All rights are reserved.

Creative Thinking Activity
Product Assessment

THE WORKPLACE COLLAGE

Directions:

For this project you will need old magazines/newspapers, markers, and large pieces of poster board, drawing paper, or newsprint. Create a collage that represents what you have learned in your study of the world of work. Consider your level of school success as a determinant of your success as an entry level worker. First review what you have learned about the world of work. Next, reflect on how our efforts to achieve school success will impact your entry into the world of work. Cut out words and pictures from magazine and newspaper headlines and use markers to insert key words and phrases where appropriate. Use the blank space below to sketch, outline, and write in some ideas to be graphically portrayed as visual images in the collage.

Creative Thinking Activity
Suggestions for Success

SCHOOL SUCCESS IS NO ACCIDENT

Directions:

Quickly read the thirty tips for school success. Go back over the list, taking time to think carefully about each item. Make a star beside each item that you feel you excel in, a check mark beside the ones that you feel you are average in, and an x beside the ones you need to work on. If you have more x's than stars, and an overabundance of check marks, take time now to re-evaluate and make plans to use your time and resources more effectively in order to pursue school success.

1. Organize your notebook. Make tabs for every subject area plus exploratory and special projects.

2. Add a daily planner to your notebook. Note exams and extracurricular dates.

3. Collect and organize your "school tools" (paper, pens, pencils, paper clips, markers, etc.).

4. Sharpen your pencils and add a pocket pencil sharpener to your "tool box."

5. Use different colored highlighters to underline important facts, color code projects, add bullets to outlines, and differentiate chart and graph facts.

6. Find a quiet and comfortable place to complete homework assignments.

7. Learn to take and use good class notes.

8. Ask your teacher to clarify anything that is unclear to you.

9. Secure a dictionary and thesaurus to be constant companions.

10. Find a "study buddy" to brainstorm, exchange notes, and study with. The person who said, "Two heads are better than one" was not all wrong.

11. Learn to make the best possible use of your school library and/or media center.

12. Make use of good listening skills in class.

Integrating School Success & Career Readiness
©2000 by Incentive Publications, Inc. Nashville, TN.

Creative Thinking Activity
Suggestions for Success

13. Review your study skills and make notes of materials and techniques to help you make improvement in areas as needed.

14. Approach classroom instruction in a positive manner.

15. Practice asking good questions and making meaningful use of answers. It has been said that questioning is more of an art than it is a science. Learn the art of questioning.

16. Get plenty of rest and eat a proper diet to insure a high energy level.

17. Make use of charts, graphs, outlines, and other diagrams to organize information.

18. Learn to use Bloom's Taxonomy of higher-order thinking skills when planning projects or completing assignments.

19. Use an editor's guide to check all written work. Checking it twice is not a bad idea.

20. Create study guides for completing blue ribbon science and math assignments. Include glossaries, terms, symbols, etc.

21. Learn to make effective use of maps, globes, and atlases.

22. Make a habit of completing homework assignments before you are too tired.

23. Set both short and long-term goals for learning. Coordinate the two lists with high expectations for success.

24. Use bookmarks to keep up with reading or homework assignments.

25. Be a list maker. Make lists of assignments and due dates; supplies needed, books read, books to be read, and library due dates; reference sources and more.

26. Look to your teachers as primary resources. Don't be afraid to ask for help after class if you need it.

27. Make your parent or guardian a partner in your learning. Share what you are learning at school and involve them in homework or independent projects when possible.

28. Learn to use community resources such as museums, the public library, community agencies, etc.

29. Learn to use and employ available technology as appropriate; Internet, computers, CDs, etc.

30. Begin now to plan for the future. Visualize, dream, and organize.

Creative Thinking Activity
Product Challenges

TEN POSSIBLE PRODUCT CHALLENGES

1. Create a student's page on the Internet designed to inform and instruct students of your age on how to improve their study skills.

2. Construct a student or parent guide for maximizing the resources available in your community. Provide valuable information or services that contribute to school success for students of your age (including, but not limited to: libraries, museums, YMCA's or YWCA's, nature conservatories, art galleries, etc.).

3. Create a plan for weaning students of your age from over-dependence on technology such as television, video games, computer graphics, etc. Encourage leisure-reading as a substitute.

4. Prepare a consumer guide for students and teachers in your school who want to get the most for their money when purchasing school supplies, resource books, and other products and services related to school success.

5. Plan and create the first issue of a monthly newsletter based on the theme of preparation now for life-long learning. Include factual or statistical information, charts or graphs, jokes or riddles, reviews or interviews, and bibliographies or summaries of health-related publications.

6. Write an article for the school newspaper evaluating the contribution of your school's physical education and sports programs to the mental, emotional, and physical health and wellness of the students.

7. Write an essay to extol the value of a lifestyle based on a good balance of academic effort, physical activity, community involvement, and social activity to school success for students of your age.

8. Compile a directory of educational-related careers that might be of interest to you and your peers.

9. Design the ultimate schedule for homework completion based on your family's lifestyle patterns. Be specific as to where, when, and how you will study; how resources will be secured; who will check work and give needed guidance; and above all, make your plan realistic, and achievable. Keep with your personal goals for school success.

10. Devise a set of graphic organizers that will help you achieve school success. Include an organizer for each of the four core subjects (math, social studies, science, and language arts), as well as outlines, diagrams, mind maps, and lesson plans that may be used for either individual studies or for a wide variety of content-based activities.

Integrating School Success & Career Readiness
©2000 by Incentive Publications, Inc. Nashville, TN.

Creative Thinking Activity
Business-Related Projects

TEN PRODUCT / PERFORMANCE PROJECTS

Directions:

Complete one or more of these business-related projects.

1. Create a poster to show the different forms of business advertising and offer both examples and advantages of each type.

2. Design an ideal business park that has businesses that cater to kids.

3. Pretend that each business in your community had to display a mural on its outside walls showing the type of product or service that they manufacture, sell, or distribute. Sketch or describe what the murals would look like for five top businesses in your neighborhood.

4. Construct a word finder or crossword puzzle describing many different occupations or professions. Be able to explain the difference, if any, between an occupation and a profession.

5. Create a story using these ten business-related words: profit, employee, strike, hazard, discrimination, capital, entrepreneur, salesman, product, and manager.

6. Design an alphabet book about various jobs, careers, occupations, or professions that young children will enjoy reading.

7. Pretend you are a store mannequin and create a comic strip series that tells the different things you see, feel, or hear during any given work day.

8. Imagine you have been hired to help a company design fashion wear for teenagers. Tell why you were hired and give a list of Do's and Don'ts for developing the company's line of products.

9. Assume you are going to open a second-hand store that will have children and teens as customers. Create a brochure telling what you will sell, how you will obtain items to sell, and how you will operate your business.

10. Imagine you have been a key employee of a business that makes vending machines. Your boss has ordered you to invent a whole new type of vending machine for the company. Describe what items you would sell in the machines and your sales or marketing plan for getting organizations to house and try out the machines.

Creative Thinking Activity
Career Education Showcase

SIX PERFORMANCES TO SHOWCASE WHAT YOU HAVE LEARNED ABOUT CAREER EDUCATION

1. Work with a small group of peers and assume the roles of a working parent, stepparent, or guardian. Use his or her resumés to find out about each worker's accomplishments. Pool all of the individual resumés to come up with a group resumé. To do this, record the following information from each resumé and combine them for a total picture of the group's job success: Educational background, positions held, major accomplishments, total years of work experience, and hobbies/talents/travel/family.

2. Work with a partner to create a series of thirty to sixty-second commercials that advertise and celebrate the essential facts and figures for a wide range of career options. Make certain that each commercial includes a logo, slogan, jingle, musical selection, and/or promotional gimmick.

3. Prepare a set of fact cards that contain several statements about the world of work — half of which are true and half of which are false. Write each statement on a separate index card and make an answer key. Share these with classmates and have peers determine which statements are true and which are false. Ask them to give reasons for their choices.

4. Organize a group of "student experts" on several different occupations or career clusters. Inform each "student expert" that his/her session will be conducted like a press conference. In keeping with the format, the "expert" is to prepare a few brief remarks or an opening statement and then be prepared to answer questions from "the press." Encourage students in the class to prepare a series of questions they would like to ask these "expert students" before their scheduled appearances.

5. Plan a program similar to the old television show, "What's My Line," which features a number of special guests with unusual jobs or work-related experiences. Ask each mystery guest to reveal his or her unique job, skill, experience, or event to the general audience while a group of panelists take turns asking "yes" or "no" questions of the mystery guest until one of the panelists is able to identify the guest's secret.

6. Select a work-related issue that has several sides to it. Divide the participants into several sub-groups — one group representing each of the different sides. Give each sub-group time to develop a list of arguments supporting their respective positions. Bring the subgroups together once again and explain that any participant from one group can begin a debate. After the first person has presented one (and only one) argument defending the pre-determined position, a different argument or counter-argument can be offered from a member of another sub-group. The discussion is continued following this format until all ideas from all groups have been exhausted. Summaries of each sub-group's position should be shared at the conclusion of the debate.

Creative Thinking Activity
Career Book Creation

TEN CAREER BOOK PROJECTS TO CREATE

1. Compile a mini-encyclopedia of several different careers by writing a simple but informative one-page report for each one. Arrange them in alphabetical order and place them in a 3-hole binder. Include a table of contents, a title page, and a cover for your mini-encyclopedia.

2. Create a pop-out book about a career of your choice. Write a fact with a brief paragraph explaining more about the fact on each page. Create a simple object or figure for each page that is glued to the top of that page with an accordion-pleated strip. As each page is turned, the object jumps out at the reader.

3. Design a quiz flap book about the world of work that discusses several different work-related concepts. Each page should ask a question that is written on the front half of a smaller piece of paper glued to the page of the book. Fold that piece of paper in half and write the answer to the question on the inside or flip side of the paper piece.

4. Write an unfolding book of career or work-related terms. Take a big piece of paper and fold it back and forth accordion style. On each section of the folded paper, write a term or vocabulary word followed by its dictionary definition.

5. Create an unrolling or scroll-type book of illustrations, diagrams, charts, or drawings that relate information about a job you have researched. Let the visuals and graphics relate most of the information rather than sentences and paragraphs of copy.

6. Write a tri-fold book using poster board or oak tag about a career of the future. Fold both ends of the poster board or oak tag into the center, which is called a gatefold. Write your report and staple it to the inside of the folder in the center area. Create a front cover for one of the tri-folds and an illustration on the other one of the tri-folds.

7. Design a file folder book. On the front side of the file folder, prepare a cover/title page. On the inside front of the file folder, write a one page report describing a special career or occupation you have learned about. On the inside of the back of the file folder, include a drawing, diagram, chart, graph, or illustration about the career. Prepare a short quiz about the given information and glue it on the backside of the file folder.

8. Design a newspaper book that describes a career or occupation from many different perspectives and types of writing. Print your information on a large piece of newsprint that is divided into columns, newspaper style. Give your newspaper a name and divide the king-size front page into several sections. Include a feature story, a news story, an editorial or letter to the editor, a display ad, a classified ad, and a comic strip — all of which convey information about the career or occupation under discussion.

9. Create a learning log or journal that records all types of factual information from your research on careers and career opportunities. Date every entry and record the source for information discussed in the various entries.

10. Design an activity book that contains a wide range of tasks about various jobs and careers. Include word finder and crossword puzzles, riddles to solve, jokes to read, mazes to figure out, hidden pictures to decipher, questions to answer, and codes to crack.

Creative Thinking Activity
Career Journal

SUGGESTED JOURNAL TOPICS

ACTIVITY ONE: Browse through the classified job ads for your local newspaper or another newspaper such as The Wall Street Journal. Clip out a variety of ads that appeal to you and create a "practice" letter of application for several of them.

ACTIVITY TWO: Create a professional resumé for yourself. Include contact information; social security number; special skills and talents; special interests and hobbies; previous work experiences; school subjects taken and grades earned; special awards; extracurricular activities; personal references; and the type of job you are most interested in.

ACTIVITY THREE: Create a timeline and/or itinerary of the ideal work week for you beginning with 8:00 a.m. on Monday morning and ending with evening hours on Friday.

ACTIVITY FOUR: Pretend it is seventy years into the future. Create the obituary about your work accomplishments that might appear in the local newspaper as well as a tombstone that might appear in your burial space.

ACTIVITY FIVE: Invent the ideal job for you, with complete specifications. Be sure to include job interests, work responsibilities, working conditions, earnings/benefits, interpersonal environment, physical space, and special circumstances/opportunities/goals.

ACTIVITY SIX: Research several of the following job education and training options available to students in your community upon graduation from high school. Compile an annotated list of these resources:

1. Vocational education
2. Non-collegiate post-secondary vocational education
3. Employer training
4. Apprenticeship programs
5. Federal employment and training programs
6. Armed Forces training
7. Home study and correspondence schools
8. Community and junior colleges
9. Colleges and universities

ACTIVITY SEVEN: Arrange to interview a successful businessperson in your community. Prepare a set of questions in advance of the interview, tape record the interview (with permission, of course), and write up the results of the interview. Don't forget to send a thank-you note to the interviewee!

Brainstorming Activity
Teams in the Workplace

COMMUNICATION COUNTDOWN

Description:

Teaming in the workplace is essential to the success of most businesses and services. As a member of a team, every individual should be aware of how they are communicating with one another. Work with a small group of peers and ask each group member to give everyone else a "grade" from 1 (low) to 5 (high) for each of the communication areas listed below and, if possible, cite actual examples to support their grades. To prepare for this activity, brainstorm a list of situations, tasks, assignments, or settings where communication of all types is required.

1. STRUCTURE: How well do I organize my messages?
2. CLARITY: How clear do I usually make myself?
3. CONCISENESS: Do I keep my messages both accurate and brief?
4. COMPLETENESS: Do I give all of the information that I should?
5. CONCRETENESS: How well do I stick to the facts?
6. CONGRUENCY: Does my body language match my words?
7. FACTUAL FEEDBACK: How well do I ensure that accurate communication has taken place?
8. FEELING FEEDBACK: How effectively do I empathize with others?

Self-Assessment Activity
Interview / Performance Assessment

INTERVIEWS ARE IMPORTANT

Description:

There is both an art and a science to job interviewing. One cannot begin learning these skills too soon. Many students in middle and high school are seeking part time jobs either informally in the neighborhood or community (if less than 16 years of age) or more formally in the workplace (if 16 years of age or older).

Review the Ten Tips For A Successful Job Interview Experience (listed below) and then complete the exercise on page 190 that lists twelve questions for you to answer in preparation for a mock job interview situation. Then, work with a partner and stage an interview simulation where one of you conducts the interview as an employer and the other responds to the interview as an employee. Ask your partner to help you assess your understanding of and ability to carry out a successful interview. Re-think your preparation for the interview process and determine what you would do differently next time.

1. Invest in the proper clothing and accessories so that your dress makes you look and feel successful.

2. Make it a point to do your homework so that you know more about the employer than he/she knows about you.

3. Simplify the interview process by communicating clearly what you have to offer and being prepared to answer questions about your personal experiences and skills.

4. Remember that employers want to hire someone for the job and you may very well be that individual.

5. Create a series of mental pictures or visual representations of yourself operating at peak performance in the job.

6. Role-play and rehearse with friends or adult advocates so they can give you practice and feedback as needed.

7. Make notes on 3 x 5 index cards of questions you want to ask and answers you want to record.

8. Remind yourself that it is all right to be nervous on such an occasion, as a little stage fright or stress often leads to a better performance.

9. Give yourself enough room and time for the interview. Don't schedule yourself so tightly that there is little "wiggle room" to allow for emergencies or extenuating circumstances.

10. Address the interviewer formally and speak the interviewer's language. Demonstrate good listening skills as well.

Creative Thinking Activity
Career Clusters

SELF-HELP OPTIONS FOR LOOKING AT CAREER CLUSTERS

Directions:

Consider each of the following methods for improving one's understanding of a career cluster. Record an advantage (or disadvantage) and a benefit (or problem area) for each of the options listed below from your perspective as a student investigator.

1. Conduct an action research project with your group of peers.
   COMMENTS: _____

2. Observe an adult performing in the workplace.
   COMMENTS: _____

3. Plan and critique an interview with a worker or business leader.
   COMMENTS: _____

4. Conduct research or visit career websites on the Internet.
   COMMENTS: _____

5. Give a presentation before an audience of peers sharing the results of your career research and findings.
   COMMENTS: _____

6. Read magazine or journal articles on the career cluster of your choice. Try writing a related article of your own.
   COMMENTS: _____

7. Maintain a reading log or learning journal. Record your thoughts, questions, observations and reflections while studying the topic.
   COMMENTS: _____

PORTFOLIO RUBRIC

RATING SCALE
1 = I could have done better
2 = I did a good job
3 = I did a terrific job

1. Organization and completeness of portfolio   1   2   3
2. Quality of artifacts selected   1   2   3
3. Creativity shown in work   1   2   3
4. Correctness of work (grammar, spelling, sentence structure, neatness, punctuation, etc.)   1   2   3
5. Evidence of learning concepts and/or applying skills   1   2   3
6. Reflection process   1   2   3
7. Evidence of enthusiasm and interest in assignments   1   2   3
8. Oral presentation of portfolio   1   2   3

```
GRADING SCALE
22–24 Points = A
18–21 Points = B
14–17 Points = C
10–13 Points = D
Under 10 Points = Unacceptable
```

My personal evaluation and comments: _____
_____
_____
_____
_____

Name: _____

Date: _____

Integrating School Success & Career Readiness
©2000 by Incentive Publications, Inc. Nashville, TN.

RUBRIC FOR ASSESSING THE QUALITY OF AN INDEPENDENT OR GROUP PROJECT, PRODUCT, OR PERFORMANCE

RATING SCALE
1 = I could have done better
2 = I did a good job
3 = I did a terrific job

1. Overall planning and organization   1   2   3

2. Quality of tasks and activities planned   1   2   3

3. Use of a variety of media and materials   1   2   3

4. Creativity and originality of work   1   2   3

5. Neatness and attention to detail shown in work   1   2   3

6. Quality of written work (grammar, punctuation, vocabulary usage, sentence structure, etc.)   1   2   3

7. Evidence of sufficient understanding of concepts and facts   1   2   3

8. Efficient use of basic language and problem solving skills   1   2   3

9. Attractive format, graphics, and presentation   1   2   3

10. Evidence of review and reflection process   1   2   3

11. Enthusiasm and excitement   1   2   3

12. Summary and presentation   1   2   3

Reflection Activity
Student Sheet

THE ABC'S OF WHAT I'VE LEARNED ABOUT THE WORLD OF WORK

Directions:

Think back over everything you have learned about the world of work, careers, and business. Write down a fact, opinion, or term definition for each letter of the alphabet listed below. Underline the key word in the fact, opinion, or definition that is the focus for each letter.

A. _____

B. _____

C. _____

D. _____

E. _____

F. _____

G. _____

H. _____

I. _____

J. _____

Integrating School Success & Career Readiness
©2000 by Incentive Publications, Inc. Nashville, TN.

Reflection Activity
Student Sheet

K. _____

L. _____

M. _____

N. _____

O. _____

P. _____

Q. _____

R. _____

S. _____

T. _____

U. _____

V. _____

W. _____

X. _____

Y. _____

Z. _____

A SUPER-PRACTICAL APPENDIX TO INTEGRATE SCHOOL SUCCESS AND CAREER READINESS

Job Fields to Consider	208
Fourteen Suggestions for Parent Involvement In Helping Schools Prepare Tomorrow's Workers	209
Planning a Career Day for Your School	210
Conduct a Company Scavenger Hunt (Exploring Community Businesses)	211
Competencies and Skills Identified in the SCANS Report	212–213
Things to Think and Talk About	214
Tasks to Try and Tell About	214
Possible Reference Findings on Work/Career Topic	215–218
Bibliography	219–221
Index	222–223

JOB FIELDS TO CONSIDER

Accounting
Activist
Administrative
Advertising
Air Conditioning
Airline
Alarm
Amusement
Appliance
Architectural
Art
Assembly
Attorney
Audio Visual
Automotive
Aviation
Bakery
Banking
Barber
Beauty
Bookkeeping
Buyer
Cabinetry
Cable
Carpentry
Carpet
Carwash
Cashier
Catering
Cellular
Chemistry
Childcare
Chiropractic
Cleaning Services
Clerical
Collections
Communications
Computer/IT
Construction
Consulting
Contract
Convention
Counseling

Courier
Craft
Credit
Custodial
Customer Service
Data Entry
Dental
Design
Dispatcher
Display
Distribution
Drafting
Drilling
Driver
Dry Cleaning
Education
Electrical
Electronics
Engineering
Environmental
Event
Financial
Fire
Fitness/Health
Floor Covering
Floral
Food Service
Forestry
Fund-raising
Furniture
General Office
Geologist
Golf
Government
Grocery
Groundskeeping
Hairstylist
Horticultural
Hotel/Motel
Human Resources
HVAC
Import/Export
Industrial

Installation
Insurance
Interior Design
Inventory
Investigation
Janitorial
Jeweler
Laboratory
Laborer
Landscaping
Law Environment
Leasing
Legal
Library
Locksmith
Logistics
Machine
Mailroom
Maintenance
Management
Manufacturing
Marketing
Meat-cutter
Mechanical
Medical
Mortgage
Movers
Musical
Newspaper
Nursing
Nutrition
Optical
Painting
Parking
Pawn Broker
Pest Control
Pet
Pharmacy
Photo
Plastics
Plumbing
Printing
Production

Property Management
Psychology
Public Relations
Publishing
Purchasing
Quality
Radio
Real Estate
Receptionist
Recreation
Refrigeration
Research
Restaurant
Retail
Roofing
Safety
Sales
Science
Secretarial
Security
Sewing
Sheet Metal
Shipping
Social Services
Statistician
Stockbroker
Surveying
Swimming
Technical
Technician
Tele-Communications
Telemarketing
Television
Textile
Training
Transportation
Travel
Veterinary
Video
Wallpaper
Warehouse
Welding
Word Processing

FOURTEEN SUGGESTIONS FOR PARENT INVOLVEMENT IN HELPING SCHOOLS PREPARE TOMORROW'S WORKERS

The following list suggests 14 ways that parents might serve as partners in the school's efforts to provide the greatest level of success for every student. While every suggestion will not be appropriate for any given situation, several should fit any one. Select the ones that fit the unique needs of your school community.

1. Start an extracurricular and after-school club in a special interest area you might have, such as photography or hiking.

2. Organize a brown bag literary club that meets monthly to discuss fiction and non-fiction bestseller books during the lunch hour.

3. Share your personal story with a group of students. Tell about your work experiences, your travels, your hobbies, or your unforgettable characters.

4. Offer to use your home computer to design and print classroom greeting cards, awards, or newsletters.

5. Organize a Cultural Events Committee and make arrangements for exhibits, musicals, art shows, and historical showcases to visit the school throughout the year.

6. Be the researcher for the teacher and use the Internet to download information on requested topics.

7. Volunteer to do the bulletin boards on a monthly or quarterly basis.

8. Organize a Publishing Center in the media center to type and bind reports, essays, and books for students without access to computers.

9. Offer to serve as the class photographer and take pictures of key events throughout the year and put them in a keepsake album.

10. Serve as the school's political "eyes and ears," keeping the staff abreast of the latest educational issues and pending legislation.

11. Organize a talent show for the school that involves students, staff, and parents as performers.

12. Organize a "meet and greet" program for the school's new families modeled after the successful community "welcome wagon" concept.

13. Serve as the public relations person for the school and develop a marketing plan to report on the school's many educational programs and offerings to the public.

14. Collect artifacts and free materials from businesses in the area and donate them to the school. Find resources in the community that teachers need to enhance their special units or projects.

PLANNING A CAREER DAY FOR YOUR SCHOOL

PURPOSE:

To explore a wide variety of career options through a special day during the school year that has been set aside to present multi-sources of information ranging from displays and exhibits to presentations and workplace products.

PROCEDURE

1. Discuss the concept of "career day" with many different groups of people including students, teachers, parents/guardians, guidance counselors, school administrators, community workers, and other adults involved with today's workplace. Brainstorm a list of "career day" activities that could be included as part of this special event.

2. Form a Career Day Committee with representatives from each of the preceding stakeholder groups. Prepare a timeline of committee meetings complete with agendas and expected outcomes for each session. Decide on a date, time, and place for the "career day" at the first committee meeting along with plans for marketing the event with the school and the public.

3. Discuss ways the following activities could be incorporated into the "career day" experience:

    A. Exhibits of career clusters

    B. Formal presentations by business employers and employees

    C. Demonstrations by community workers on what they do and how they do it

    D. Skits or role-plays by students on such topics as interview techniques and resumé writing

    E. Displays of the latest work-related tools, technology, and products

    F. Clean-up committee whose job it is to return things back to normal

4. Organize a series of sub-committees to plan and orchestrate the following tasks to make the "career day" a big success:

    A. Public relations or marketing committee whose job it is to advertise the "career day."

    B. Invitation and decorating committee whose job it is to extend multiple invitations to guests and decorate the facilities with a careers theme.

    C. Food committee whose job it is to plan and obtain refreshments to be served or sold.

    D. Program committee whose job it is to plan and print a formal program of special events.

    E. Host and hostess committee whose job it is to greet the guests and escort them around the facility on a need basis.

    F. Clean-up committee whose job it is to return things back to normal.

EVALUATION

Plan some type of meaningful feedback process for determining whether the "career day" was a success or not and what might be done better or differently next time. Consider surveys, questionnaires, observation checklists, or interviews for this task.

Exploring Community Businesses

CONDUCT A COMPANY SCAVENGER HUNT

Directions:

Work with a small group of your peers to investigate many different types of companies and businesses that operate in your community. Visit or contact each of these businesses by telephone, mail, or in person and obtain some type of descriptive artifact (brochure, annual report, advertising mailer, business card, catalog, etc.) to share with other members of the class.

1. Try locating a company within your community that produces an unusual product.

2. Try locating a company within your community that offers a not-so-common service.

3. Try locating a company within your community that has been in business for over 25 years.

4. Try locating a company within your community that is new and less than a year old.

5. Try locating a company within your community that is operated out of the home.

6. Try locating a company within your community that has less than five employees.

7. Try locating a company within your community that has over one hundred employees.

8. Try locating a company within your community that is on the New York Stock Exchange.

9. Try locating a company within your community that sells products or provides services only through the Internet.

10. Try locating a company within your community that is owned by a minority.

11. Try locating a company within your community that you would like to go to work for.

12. Try locating a company within your community that deals with environmental products or issues.

Integrating School Success & Career Readiness
©2000 by Incentive Publications, Inc. Nashville, TN.

COMPETENCIES AND SKILLS IDENTIFIED IN THE SCANS REPORT

DESCRIPTION:

The Labor Secretary's Commission on Achieving Necessary Skills (SCANS) was asked to examine the demands of the workplace and whether our young people are capable of meeting those demands. Specifically, the Commission was asked to: (1) define the skills needed for employment; (2) propose acceptable levels of proficiency; (3) suggest effective ways to assess proficiency; and (4) develop a dissemination strategy for the nation's schools, businesses, and homes. The five SCANS competencies span the chasm between school and the workplace. SCANS research verifies that what we call workplace know-how defines effective job performance today. This know-how has two elements: "competencies" and a "foundation of basic skills." In essence, these sets of five competencies along with the three sets of skill areas are hallmarks of today's expert worker.

FIVE COMPETENCIES

RESOURCES: Identifies, organizes, plans, and allocates resources.
  a. Time. Selects goal-relevant activities, ranks them, allocates time, and prepares and follows schedules.
  b. Money. Uses or prepares budgets, makes forecasts, keeps records, and makes adjustments to meet objectives.
  c. Material and Facilities. Acquires, stores, allocates, and uses materials or space efficiently.
  d. Human Resources. Assesses skills and distributes work accordingly, evaluates performance, and provides feedback.

INTERPERSONAL: Works with others.
  a. Participates as Member of a Team. Contributes to group effort.
  b. Teaches Others New Skills.
  c. Serves Clients/Customers. Works to satisfy customers' expectations.
  d. Exercises Leadership. Communicates ideas to justify position, persuades and convinces others, responsibly challenges existing procedures and policies.
  e. Negotiates. Works toward agreements involving exchanges of resources, resolves divergent interests.
  f. Works with Diversity. Works well with men and women from diverse backgrounds.

INFORMATION: Acquires and uses information.
  a. Acquires And Evaluates Information.
  b. Organizes And Maintains Information.
  c. Interprets And Communicates Information.
  d. Uses Computers to Process Information.

SYSTEMS: Understands complex inter-relationships.
  a. Understands Systems. Knows how social, organizational, and technological systems work and operates effectively with them.
  b. Monitors And Corrects Performance. Distinguishes trends, predicts impacts on system operations, diagnoses deviations in system's performance, and corrects malfunctions.
  c. Improves or Designs Systems. Suggests modifications to existing systems and develops new or alternative systems to improve performance.

TECHNOLOGY: Works with a variety of technologies.
  a. Selects Technology. Chooses procedures, tools, or equipment, including computers and related technologies.
  b. Applies Technology to Task. Understands overall intent and proper procedures for setup and operation of equipment.
  c. Maintains and Troubleshoots Equipment. Prevents, identifies, or solves problems with equipment, including computers and other technologies.

FOUNDATION SKILLS IDENTIFIED IN THE SCANS REPORT

BASIC SKILLS: Reads, writes, performs arithmetic and mathematical operations, listens and speaks.
  a. Reading. Locates, understands, and interprets written information in prose and in documents such as manuals, graphs, and schedules.
  b. Writing. Communicates thoughts, ideas, information, and messages in writing and creates documents such as letters, directions, manuals, reports, graphs, and flowcharts.
  c. Arithmetic/mathematics. Performs basic computations and approaches practical problems by choosing appropriately from a variety of mathematical techniques.
  d. Listening. Receives, attends to, interprets, and responds to verbal messages and other cues.
  e. Speaking. Organizes ideas and communicates orally.

THINKING SKILLS: Thinks creatively, makes decisions, solves problems, visualizes, knows how to learn, and reasons.
  a. Creative Thinking. Generates new ideas.
  b. Decision Making. Specifies goals and constraints, generates alternatives, considers risks, and evaluates and chooses best alternative.
  c. Problem Solving. Recognizes problems and devises and implements plan of action.
  d. Seeing Things in the Mind's Eye. Organizes and processes symbols, pictures, graphs, objects, and other information.
  e. Knowing How to Learn. Uses efficient learning techniques to acquire and apply new knowledge and skills.
  f. Reasoning. Discovers a rule or principle underlying the relationship between two or more objects and applies it when solving a problem.

PERSONAL QUALITIES: Displays responsibility, self-esteem, sociability, self-management, integrity, and honesty.
  a. Responsibility. Exerts a high level of effort and perseveres towards goal attainment.
  b. Self-Esteem. Believes in own self-worth and maintains a positive view of self.
  c. Sociability. Demonstrates understanding, friendliness, adaptability, empathy, and politeness in group settings.
  d. Self-management. Assesses self accurately, sets personal goals, monitors progress, and exhibits self-control.
  e. Integrity/Honesty. Chooses ethical courses of action.

SOURCE: U.S. Department of Labor, Secretary's Commission on Achieving Necessary Skills. (1991, June). What work requires of schools: A SCANS report for America 2000. Washington, D.C.: Government Printing Office. xviii.

Things to Think and Talk About

1. Why do you think the Labor Secretary's Commission on Achieving Necessary Skills (SCANS) was asked to examine the demands of today's workplace and whether our young people are capable of meeting those demands?

2. Who stands to benefit from this SCANS report?

3. What do we mean by the notion of "competencies?" How do we tell whether someone is competent or not in each of the five competency areas identified in the SCANS report?

4. Why are "basic skills," "thinking skills," and "personal qualities" considered to be the foundation skills required for success in the workplace?

5. How could the SCANS report best be used as a resource in schools today?

Tasks to Try and Tell About

1. Analyze the Five Competencies and determine in which areas you have the greatest strengths and the most obvious weaknesses.

2. Analyze the Three Basic Skill Foundation areas and determine in which areas you have the greatest strengths and the most obvious weaknesses.

3. Compare and contrast each of your core curricular classes (Math, English, Social Studies, and Science) to find out which competencies are best covered in each course.

4. Compare and contrast each of your core curricular classes (Math, English, Social Studies, and Science) to find out which foundation skill areas are best covered in each course.

5. Prepare an outline to suggest ways that an Advisory Program could incorporate several of the ideas suggested in the SCANS report as part of its curriculum and classroom sessions.

Work / Career Topic

POSSIBLE REFERENCE FINDINGS ON WORK/CAREER TOPIC

(FROM WORK AS CONTENT POINT OF VIEW)

CHAPTER ONE: Ronald L. Krannich & Caryl Rae Krannich emphasize:
The first step in finding a job that is right for any individual involves assessing one's skills, abilities, motivations, interests, values, temperaments, experiences, and accomplishments. A person's strategy is to develop a firm foundation of information on oneself before proceeding to other stages in the career development process. This self-assessment develops the necessary self-awareness upon which one can effectively communicate his/her qualifications to employers as well as focus and build one's career.
    SOURCE: Krannich, R. L. & Krannich, C. R. (1993) *Discover The Best Jobs For*
    You. Manassas Park, VA: Impact Publications. p. 55.

CHAPTER TWO: Per Dalin writes:
There are three basic learning needs that most students have today as they face the future:

1. BASIC KNOWLEDGE AND SKILLS are increasingly important, but what is basic? Learning how to learn, understanding the characteristics of each discipline, mastering open problem-solving, and learning to communicate. These needs can best be achieved if we realize fully that the school culture is a community where we can draw on a number of learning resources in the school and in the community.

2. KNOWLEDGE AND UNDERSTANDING are not the same. Knowledge is still important; however we have much knowledge in our world and little understanding. "Deep knowledge" is the goal; we must help our students to "put the pieces of information together," to internalize knowledge so that they "own" it. This can best be achieved through "authentic" learning experiences, where the student has full responsibility and learns to develop empathy for others.

3. CONSUMER AND PRODUCER: We are all, and we shall always be, consumers. Facing the dramatic challenges to our way of living we need to become more critical consumers, to reflect principles of the environment, health, and equity goals. Fewer of us, however, are "producers," or use our creative talent in the formation of our societies in the work place, at home, in the local environment, and in the media. Most of what we do in schools is reproduction rather than production, and little time is used to reflect and to discuss the value choices we face.
    SOURCE: Dalin, Per. "Can Schools Learn? Preparing for the 21st Century,"
    Bulletin, NASSP, Vol. 80, No. 576, January, 1996, p.12.

CHAPTER THREE: Lawrence K Jones states:
Yes, you have been studying basic skills like reading and mathematics for years, but do you know how these skills are used on a job? Often workers use these skills in different ways than students do. Workers today spend an average of two hours a day reading such things as letters, records, tables, charts, directories, manuals, and computer terminals. They read to get the information they need to do their work. You will need to read for details, and to do it rapidly and accurately. You will also need strong writing skills. In your work you will want to describe what you observe, state your opinions, and ask questions. You will request, explain, illustrate, and convince. It is important that you do these things clearly, rapidly, completely, and accurately, both on paper and with a computer.

Work / Career Topic

Likewise, you will speak with many people each day at work. In talking with co-workers or customers, you may explain how something works, or describe procedures to be followed. You may ask questions to identify why something is not working, or speak in a way that will encourage co-workers to express themselves fully. It is important to do this clearly and effectively.

Finally, you will spend most of your working day communicating over the telephone with co-workers, customers, and your supervisor. Your ability to communicate through reading, writing, speaking, and listening will determine your job success. Only the knowledge of your job is more important than communication skills in predicting your job success. Employers value communication skills. They know that such skills are at the heart of getting and keeping customers, and of workers working. Of the time the average worker spends communicating, most frequent activities are speaking (23%) and listening (55%).
    SOURCE: *Jones, L. K. (1996) Job Skills For The 21st Century. Phoenix: Oryx Press,*
       pp. 51, 55, 63, & 65.

CHAPTER FOUR: Arnold H. Packer and Marion W. Pines conclude:
Various traditional programs have sought to provide school age youth with meaningful workplace experience. Cooperative education is the most long-established and widespread attempt to coordinate work and school. School-based coordinators enroll employers and make the connections. Students work for pay, usually close to the minimum wage. On the other hand, many students find work through agricultural education. Apprentice relationships with employers are not a necessary, or even common, part of these agricultural programs. School-based enterprises, where the school operates a business or activity, comprise still another mode of creating work-based learning without directly involving employers. Students working in these enterprises often have an opportunity to become entrepreneurs and apply the skills and knowledge learned in their academic courses. Finally, students volunteer for community service roles, from candy stripers in hospitals to food dispensers at soup kitchens, often exploring career options.
    SOURCE: *Packer, A. H. & Pines, M. W. (1996) School-To-Work. Princeton: Eye On*
       Education, pp. 41 and 43.

CHAPTER FIVE: Bob Nelson discovers:
According to Bob Nelson, Kimberly Smithson, marketing manager of Motivation Online in Hoffman Estates, Illinois offers the following tips on how to be creative on the job:

1. BRAINSTORMING: The goal of brainstorming is to develop as many ideas as possible; not to critique, analyze, or discuss them or to make decisions. Create a chart and list as many ideas on a topic as possible. Some of the ideas may be pretty ridiculous, but everything goes on the list. The psychological principle behind brainstorming is called triggering. Any idea, no matter how dumb it seems, can trigger a viable idea.
2. PARE IT DOWN: Most people think that in order to be creative, you have to invent something new. You can be just as creative by getting rid of things. By eliminating the unnecessary, you can improve processes and ways of doing things.
3. MODIFY WHAT EXISTS: By modifying something you already have, you may come up with something new, different, or better. You can also get many good ideas by observing things around you. If you adapt what you observe in one context of your life, you may be able to solve a problem you face in another situation.
4. LATERAL THINKING: Most of the time when you face a problem, you attack it logically and that's good. However, what's logical may not be the only approach. Often the answer to a problem is not right in front of you, but can be found by looking at it from a different angle.

    SOURCE: *Nelson, B. (1999) 1001 Ways To Take Initiative At Work. New York:*
       Workman Publishing, pp. 10, 11.

Work / Career Topic

CHAPTER SIX: William Edwards Deming summarizes:
I encourage educators to create school environments in which strong relationships of mutual respect and trust replace fear, suspicion, and division; and in which leadership from administrators and policymakers empowers students and teachers (as front-line workers of the school) to make continuous improvements in the work they do together. The development of everyone's "yearning for learning" is all-important in Schools of Quality; grades and other symbols of learning are far less significant. The school, says Deming, should be a place where students, teachers, administrators, and others are able to take pride and joy in their work. It is the responsibility of administrators, the top management of schools, to remove the barriers that prevent this from being the daily experience of students and teachers.
SOURCE: *Bonstingl, J. J. (1992) Schools of Quality. Alexandria, VA: Association for Supervision and Curriculum Development pp. 18–19.*

(FROM INSTRUCTIONAL STRATEGY POINT OF VIEW)

CHAPTER ONE: Linda Campbell and others write:
Dr. Howard Gardner, Co-Director of Project Zero and Professor of Education at Harvard University, has for many years conducted research on the development of human cognitive capacities. He has broken from the common tradition of intelligence theory that adheres to two fundamental assumptions: that cognition is unitary and that individuals can be adequately described as having a single, quantifiable intelligence. In his study of human capacities, Gardner established criteria to measure whether a talent was actually intelligence. Each intelligence must have a developmental feature, be observable in special populations such as prodigies or "idiots savants," provide some evidence of localization in the brain, and support a symbolic or notational system.

Gardner's research revealed a wider family of human intelligences than previously believed, and offered a refreshingly pragmatic definition of intelligence. Instead of viewing "smartness" in terms of a score on a standardized test, Gardner defines intelligence as:
. . . The ability to solve problems that one encounters in real life.
. . . The ability to generate new problems to solve.
. . . The ability to make something or offer a service that is valued within one's culture.
This definition of intelligence underscores the multicultural nature of Gardner's theory.
SOURCE: *Campbell, L. etc. (1999) Teaching & Learning Through Multiple Intelligences. Needham Heights, MA: Allyn and Bacon, p. xv.*

CHAPTER TWO: Mary Louise Hawkins and M. Dolores Graham conclude:
Authors of education texts have a field day defining curriculum. The definitions vary widely, although they usually define curriculum as more than the combined courses of study. In many ways it may be more helpful to start here by defining what curriculum is not.
1. The curriculum is not a collection of textbooks.
2. The curriculum is not revision.
3. The curriculum is not a sequenced list of skills and competencies.
4. The curriculum is not a course guide of prerequisites and course titles.
5. The curriculum is not scope and sequence.
6. The curriculum is not the teacher's preference.

Curriculum is a plan to engage students in learning. These words suggest that curriculum is a set of decisions that planners make about how to access resources, activities, facilities, previous experience, and make connections with other learning. Planners may be teachers, students, or a combination of the two. The quality of the plan is measured by how well students can engage in learning by being involved.
SOURCE: *Hawkins, M. L. & Graham, M. D. (1994) Curriculum Architecture, Columbus, OH: National Middle School Association, pp.42–43.*

Work / Career Topic

CHAPTER THREE: Jon Saphier and Robert Gower stress:
For students of teaching, few other efforts are as rewarding and as challenging as learning new models of teaching. Even the most mature and sophisticated of professionals can add to their repertoires and to their power to reach a broader range of students.

A model of teaching is a particular pattern of instruction that is recognizable and consistent; you can recognize it and label it when you see it, yet it is distinctly different from patterns in other models of teaching. A model has particular values, goals, a rationale, and an orientation to how learning shall take place (e.g., by induction, by discovery, through heightened personal awareness, by wrestling with puzzling data, or by organizing information hierarchically). That orientation is developed into a specific set of phases teachers and students go through, in order, with specific kinds of events in each phase. Each model of teaching is a particular entity with specific components, well worked out, and with markedly different appearances and effects.
  SOURCE: Saphier, J. & Gower, R. (1997) *The Skillful Teacher.* Acton, MA: Research
    For Better Teaching, Inc. p. 271.

CHAPTER FOUR: Phillip C. Schlechty discusses:
What would happen if schools were structured differently? One cannot be certain, but there are some hints. Cooperative learning (a technique of putting children in work groups and assuring that children with different backgrounds and differing abilities have experiences in working together in productive ways) has proved to be effective in developing basic skills in kids of wide ranges of background, and at the same time, developing skills in thinking, group problem solving, and so on.
  SOURCE: Schlechty, P. C. (1990) *Schools For The 21st Century.* San Francisco, CA:
    Jossey-Bass Publishers, p. 41.

CHAPTER FIVE: Paul George, Gordon Lawrence, and Donna Bushnell state:
A long time ago, Nicholas Hobbs, Provost of Vanderbilt University and a very wise teacher of teachers, and an expert teacher himself, taught his students "It is the job of the teacher to precipitate the student into just manageable difficulty." In plain talk, this means that, regardless of the ability level of the student, the truly expert teacher is one who knows the students so well and who plans so carefully that students are asked to stretch to exactly what they are capable of doing . . . no more . . . no less. That is personalizing instruction. Hobbs understood that students, all of us really, grow best when what we are asked to do matches what we are capable of doing. Our strength increases when we get in deep, but not in over our heads, in any life situation. The expert teacher helps students discover their strengths and build on them this way.
  SOURCE: George, P. & Others. (1998) *Handbook For Middle School Teaching,* New York:
    Addison-Wesley Educational Publishers, Inc. p. 490

CHAPTER SIX: Betty Lou Leaver points out:
Although accommodation of student learning style is highly encouraged, if not essential, during teaching and testing, teachers have a wonderful opportunity during periods of review to help students develop flexibility in learning styles. They do this through a variety of kinds of learning strategy training: awareness training, implicit strategy training, and explicit strategy training. Explicit strategy training is the most involved and the most effective, especially when it is long-term and regular. The value of expanding students' learning styles through strategy training is reinforced by the consideration that students who have a large inventory of learning strategies that they use appropriately are going to be better students, regardless of their so-called "academic potential."

Teachers who train their students not only in the content of their courses but in the strategies needed to live and succeed in the real world truly give their students the tools that they need to continue as lifelong learners.
  SOURCE: Leaver, B. L. (1997) *Teaching the Whole Class,* Thousand Oaks, CA:
    Corwin Press, Inc. p.163.

BIBLIOGRAPHY

An annotated bibliography of Incentive Publications titles selected to provide additional help for integrating instruction in school success and career readiness.

Breeden, Terri. Cooperative Learning Companion. Nashville, TN: Incentive Publications, 1992. (Grades 5–8). *Creative teaching aids include charts, forms, and posters. Comprehensive instructions tell how to set up an effective cooperative classroom environment.*

Breeden, Terri and Emalie Egan. Positive Classroom Management. Nashville, TN: Incentive Publications, 1997. (Grades 5–12). *This guide offers a plethora of creative, proactive ideas to make the classroom a fun, yet controlled, learning environment.*

Breeden, Terri and Emalie Egan. Strategies and Activities to Raise Achievement. Nashville, TN: Incentive Publications, 1995. (Grades 4–8). *A comprehensive manual containing high-interest activities and esteem-building exercises designed to motivate students to become more effective test-takers and successful lifelong learners.*

Connors, Neila. If You Don't Feed the Teachers They Eat the Students. Nashville, TN: Incentive Publications, 2000. (Administrators and teachers at all levels). *The emphasis of this book is on creating a positive climate, teacher motivation, and keeping schools on a winning track.*

Farnette, Cherrie, Imogene Forte, and Barbara Loss. I've Got Me and I'm Glad, Revised Edition. Nashville, TN: Incentive Publications, 1989. (Grades 4–7). *A self-awareness resource with high-interest reproducible activities designed to help kids identify their strengths and weaknesses and establish short- and long-range goals.*

Farnette, Cherrie, Imogene Forte, and Barbara Loss. People Need Each Other, Revised Edition. Nashville, TN: Incentive Publications, 1989. (Grades 4–7). *These social awareness activities were designed to build student understanding of family, peers, and the community by encouraging the use of effective communication skills.*

Forte, Imogene and Sandra Schurr. A to Z Community and Service Learning. Nashville, TN: Incentive Publications, 1997. (Middle Grades). *The research-based, fun-filled activities in this series make learning exciting and challenging. Just what busy teachers need for a dynamic, effective classroom.*

Bibliography

Forte, Imogene and Sandra Schurr. The Cooperative Learning Guide and Planning Pak for Middle Grades. Nashville, TN: Incentive Publications, 1992. (Grades 5–8). *A collection of high-interest thematic units, thematic thinking skills projects, and thematic poster projects. Includes reference skills sharpeners and much more.*

Forte, Imogene and Sandra Schurr. The Definitive Middle School Guide: A Handbook for Success. Nashville, TN: Incentive Publications, 1993. (Grades 5–8). *This comprehensive, research-based manual provides the perfect overview for educators and administrators who are determined to establish a school environment that stimulates and motivates the Middle Grade student in the learning process.*

Forte, Imogene and Sandra Schurr. Graphic Organizers and Planning Outlines. Nashville, TN: Incentive Publications, 1996. (Grades 4–8). *Eight Major sections include: Charts, Graphs, and Grids; Cognitive Taxonomy Outlines; Forms for Group Learning; Forms for Interdisciplinary Teaching; Planning Forms and Outlines; Research and Study Aids; The Web; and Writing Planners and Organizers.*

Forte, Imogene and Sandra Schurr. Interdisciplinary Units and Projects for Thematic Instruction for Middle Grade Success. Nashville, TN: Incentive Publications, 1994. (Grades 5–8). *A jumbo-sized collection of the thematic-based interdisciplinary activities and assignments that were created to spark student interest, encourage communication, and promote problem solving as well as decision making.*

Forte, Imogene and Sandra Schurr. Making Portfolios, Products, and Performances Meaningful and Manageable for Students and Teachers. Nashville, TN: Incentive Publications, 1995. (Grades 4–8). *Filled with valuable information and specific suggestions for incorporating authentic assessment techniques that help students enjoy a more active role in the evaluation process. It includes a convenient pullout Graphic Organizer with creative ideas for integrating content instruction and appraising student understanding.*

Forte, Imogene. The Me I'm Learning to Be, Rev. Ed. Nashville, TN: Incentive Publications, 1991. (Grades 4–7). *This dynamic self-awareness book provides a wealth of reproducible activity pages that focus on feelings, attitudes, and self-esteem issues.*

Forte, Imogene and Sandra Schurr. Middle Grades Advisee/Advisor Program. Nashville, TN: Incentive Publications, 1991. (Grades 5–8). *A comprehensive program dedicated to meeting the needs and confronting the challenges of today's young adolescent students. A flexible, manageable curriculum, available at three different levels, that contains both a teacher's guide and over 300 reproducible activities on essential topics.*

Forte, Imogene and Sandra Schurr. Tools, Treasures, and Measures for Middle Grade Success. Nashville, TN: Incentive Publications, 1994. (Grades 5–8). *This practical resource offers a wide assortment of teaching essentials, from ready-to-use lesson plans and student assignments to valuable lists and assessment tools.*

Forte, Imogene and Joy MacKenzie. Writing Survival Skills for the Middle Grades. Nashville, TN: Incentive Publications, 1991. (Grades 5–8). *Test taking, resumés, business letters, and job applications are just a few of the topics covered in this essential writing skills handbook.*

Frender, Gloria. Learning to Learn. Nashville, TN: Incentive Publications, 1990. (All Grades). *Creative ideas, practical suggestions, and "hands on" materials to help students acquire organizational, study, test taking, and problem solving skills needed to become lifelong effective learners.*

Frender, Gloria. Teaching for Learning Success. Nashville, TN: Incentive Publications, 1994. (Grades 5–12). *Includes practical strategies and ready-to-use materials for organizing yourself, your classroom, and your students as well as encouraging parent involvement.*

Graham, Leland and Darriel Ledbetter. How to Write a Great Research Paper. Nashville, TN: Incentive Publications, 1994. (Grades 5–8). *Mini-lessons help students choose and narrow topics, locate information, take notes, organize an outline, develop a rough draft, document sources, as well as write, revise, and evaluate their final papers.*

Heidel, John and Marion Lyman-Mersereau. Character education, Volumes One and Two, Grades 6–12. Nashville, TN: Incentive Publications, 1999. (Grades 6–12). *Values such as honesty, peace, and respect are taught through discussion questions, proverbs and maxims, activities, and stories from several religions and cultures in this two-year program. For use in a single classroom or across a school campus.*

Hibbert, Lorri and Nancy Ullinskey. Challenges and Choices. Nashville, TN: Incentive Publications, 1994. (Grades 5–8). *Nine original stories highlight sensitive issues commonly faced by adolescents. Intended for use in Advisor/Advisee programs.*

Newton, Cathy Griggs. Risk It. Nashville, TN: Incentive Publications, 1996. (Grades 4–8). *This book teaches teachers how to develop opportunities for positive risk in the classroom by presenting a comprehensive, proactive approach for delivering education that directly addresses the risk-taking behaviors of young people.*

Philpot, Jan and Ed. Partners in Learning and Growing: Linking the Home, School, and Community through Curriculum-based Programs. Nashville, TN: Incentive Publications, 1994. (Grades 5–8). *This collection of original programs is a year-long plan to foster community and parental involvement in the school and classroom.*

INDEX

Activities
    Bloom's Taxonomy 50–71
    Circle of Knowledge 159
    Cooperative Learning 139–183
    Investigation Cards 66–71
    Jigsaw 161
    Multiple Intelligences 16–28
    Read and Relate 36–38
    Round Table 149
    Team Learning 145
    Think/Pair/Share 164
    Three-step Interview 168
    Williams' Taxonomy 87

Annotated bibliography 219–221

Appendix 207–223

Assessment, authentic
    Journal writing 199
    Overview 185
    Performance 196–197
    Portfolio 203
    Product 195–196

Basic Skills
    Activities 108–138
    Overview 107

Bibliography 219–221

Bloom's Taxonomy
    Activities 50–64
    Investigation cards 66–71
    Overview 48–49

Circle of Knowledge
    Activities 159
    Instructions 143
    Prompts 160
    Student directions 159

Cooperative learning
    Activity 145–183
    Overview 140

Gardner's Multiple Intelligences
    Activities 16–28
    Overview 12–13

Investigation Cards
    Cards 67–71
    Overview 65

Jigsaw
    Activity 162
    Instructions 144
    Recording sheet 162
    Student directions 161

Journal Writing
    Reflection starter statements 199
    Springboards 46

Index

Learning Stations
    Formats 33
    Instructions 31–32
    Overview 29–30

Maslow
    Maslow's Hierarchy of Needs 26

Multiple Intelligences
    Activities 16–28
    Overview 12–13
    Planning Outline 14–15

Performances
    Assessment 197, 201
    Projects 196

Portfolio
    Rubrics 203, 204

Preface 9–10

Questions/prompts 177, 190
    Circle of Knowledge 159
    Jigsaw 161
    Round table 149

Read and Relate
    Activities 36–38
    Overview 35

Recording sheets
    Jigsaw 162
    Round Table 150
    Team Learning 146
    Think/Pair/Share 166
    Three-step Interview 169

Round Table
    Activities 149
    Instructions 144

Rubrics 203–204

Springboards for Journal Writing 46

Student Directions
    Circle of Knowledge 159
    Jigsaw 161
    Round table 149
    Team Learning 145
    Think/Pair/Share 164
    Three-step Interview 167

Student Performances 196

Student products, springboards 196

Student Reports 137

Team Learning
    Activities 146, 149
    Instructions 145

Think/Pair/Share
    Instructions 164
    Recording sheet 166

Three-step interview
    Activities 168
    Instructions 167

Topics for Student Reports 195

Williams' Taxonomy
    Activities 74–87
    Overview 72–73
    Read and Relate 35–38

Williams' Taxonomy of Creative Thought Chart 73